SENSE AND SENSITIVITY IN GYMNASTICS

SENSE AND SENSITIVITY
IN GYMNASTICS

A teacher's guide to educational gymnastics

by
Joyce E. Allen
Lecturer in Physical Education
University of Otago

HEINEMANN · LONDON

Heinemann Educational Books Ltd
LONDON EDINBURGH MELBOURNE AUCKLAND
TORONTO HONG KONG SINGAPORE KUALA LUMPUR
NEW DELHI NAIROBI JOHANNESBURG LUSAKA
IBADAN KINGSTON

ISBN 0 435 80020 5

Published by Heinemann Educational Books Ltd
48 Charles Street, London W1X 8AH
Printed Offset Litho and bound in Great Britain by
Cox & Wyman Ltd, London, Fakenham and Reading

CONTENTS

(Plates I–VIII appear between pages 40 and 41)

PREFACE

The aim of this book is to provide a guide to the methods by which the aims of Educational Gymnastics may be achieved. It is written primarily for the teacher who is inexperienced at teaching this type of work. Although written for girls, much of the material which follows could easily be used or adapted for boys' work.

I believe in the validity of the Educational Gymnastics approach at both primary and secondary school level. However, experience has taught me that no one teaching method can satisfy the constantly changing needs of *all* individuals *all the time*. It is often necessary to use a variety of teaching techniques.

I am convinced that the original educational concept can best be served through sensitive selection of appropriate teaching methods according to the ability, progress, interest and confidence of the individual or group concerned. This book attempts to stimulate teachers to consider which combinations of teaching methods may, at various stages, most effectively achieve the objectives involved in Educational Gymnastics.

I am well aware that many teachers use a variety of methods. My concern centres about those who fanatically deny the educational value of direct teaching *at any time*. Such fanaticism can, and does, erect a formidable barrier of scepticism, which causes some 'formally' trained teachers to lose any interest they may have in Educational Gymnastics. I would suggest that completely to deny the value of direct teaching is to negate the fundamental principle upon which Educational Gymnastics is founded, i.e. development of the individual *as an individual*. It is to replace one system of total formality with one of total informality. This presupposes that all individuals are the same, only in a different way. Occasionally, even the most inventive individuals appreciate direct instruction, particularly when it improves mechanical efficiency and thereby facilitates achievement. When the direct tasks outlined in this book involve a specific skill or vault, it is assumed that the correct techniques have already been taught.

University of Otago
Dunedin, N.Z.

JOYCE E. ALLEN.
January 1969

ACKNOWLEDGEMENTS

My own teaching experience, courses and demonstrations, reading, discussion with students and colleagues have all influenced and contributed to the ideas expressed in this book.

I would like to thank Mr Dudley Wills, Superintendent of Physical Education in New Zealand and members of the Physical Education Department, Wellington; Jean Silver, Senior Physical Education Adviser, Auckland; Valerie Pemberton, Lecturer in Physical Education, Ardmore Teachers' College, Auckland, for so generously giving of their time to read, appraise and correct the text.

I am indebted and most grateful to Joy Smith, Lecturer in Physical Education, University of Otago, for her fine efforts in editing and illustrating this material.

I would like to thank Miss Wood, Headmistress of St. Cuthbert's College, Auckland; Mr. Angus Howie, Technician at the School of Physical Education, University of Otago and all the students who helped to provide the photographic material.

J.E.A.

PART ONE: Fundamentals

1 Introduction

The movement research of Czechoslovakian-born Rudolf Laban, provided principles which became the scaffolding upon which Educational Gymnastics was built. Laban observed the spectrum of movement potential. 'He stressed the fact that each person possesses specific movement characteristics and a natural rhythm of moving, which enables him or her to master some movements more easily than others.'[1] His observations led him to believe that certain factors were not only common but essential to all movement. To describe the common factors, he used the terms *Time*, *Weight*, *Space* and *Flow*. These factors enable us to recognize relationships which exist between the integral parts of all movement.

In England, twenty years ago, little consideration was given to individual differences. Most people had recognized similarities in movement ability. Therefore, mass-produced exercises and vaults prevailed. Laban's observations, combined with the general climate of dissatisfaction, made it possible to re-assess the values of the existing school gymnastic programme. Gradually, Educational Gymnastics emerged. It was based on Laban's theories and encouraged creativity.

The new approach advocated the use of an informal teaching method in which actions were not specifically described. Direct teaching was replaced with a teaching method which relied upon the teacher's ability to extract movements and ideas from her class. When aiming to produce a Long-fly, the teacher could set the task, 'Get over the box using your hands only.' The result might be a Long-fly or any other movement in which weight was taken solely on hands.

The Educational Gymnastics approach attempted to provide an environment in which students could work within their own capabilities successfully to develop their own specific movement ability and characteristics. It attempted to develop independence and encouraged students to contribute to the movement content of the lesson. Uniform performance of various exercises and vaults was no longer required. The teacher was to guide students towards an awareness of the integral parts of gymnastic movement and to develop their understanding of the relationships which exist between those parts. She was required to develop the student's ability to correlate experience and independently

[1] Inner London Education Authority, *Educational Gymnastics*, London, I.L.E.A., 1965, p. 2.

1

apply knowledge to new movement problems. It was as if learning through recitation had been replaced by learning through projects. The teacher was to stimulate and guide rather than directly coach the group.

Initially, in an attempt to cast off the previously rigid gymnastic syllabus, too much emphasis was placed on extraction. Specific instruction was considered to be restricting, whilst extraction was considered to be synonymous with developing creativity. For a time, it was forgotten that even the creative dancer needs technique work! Consequently, the initial criticism levelled at the new approach, that it was too airy-fairy and vague, was disappointingly true in some cases. The new terminology and inadequately defined aims caused confusion. Staff of the 'old school' either showed scepticism or bravely attempted to modify teaching material and method. But all this was a considerable time ago.

During the past ten years, aims have been clarified and methods modified. More trained teachers, possessing a better understanding of the principles and aims involved in Educational Gymnastics have been going into schools. Conferences have stimulated discussions on points arising out of demonstration work or everyday teaching situations. Various courses have assisted the uninitiated to cope better with modifying their teaching material and approach. Gradually, teachers have exercised more control through the medium of limitation. Consequently, purposeful movements have superseded those which were irrelevantly decorative.

What's in a Name?

Teaching methods are born of educational philosophy. They reflect belief in specific educational concepts. Educational Gymnastics was later recognized as an early product of a changing attitude which was spreading throughout the whole field of education. A new philosophy was taking shape. It produced a different set of values and objectives in which the primary educational aim was the development of the student as an individual. The new objectives could not be achieved within the existing school gymnastic approach. It was necessary to develop a teaching technique which allowed flexibility. Informality, extraction and problem-solving were distinctive features of the new technique. Our philosophy determines the lesser or greater degree of educational value we may attribute to any form of gymnastics. It is regrettable that the title in which we cloak our philosophy can become more of a stumbling-block to acceptance than the educational concept itself! The very name Educational Gymnastics often evokes an understandable measure of protest and occasionally, even strong resentment. Throughout this book, I refer to Educational Gymnastics although I confess to some embarrassment concerning the word *educational*. It has been argued that any form of gymnastics is educational. Most of us would agree that each form of gymnastics has its own intrinsic value. We would recognize that each caters for a specific need and offers satisfaction to different age-groups, somatotypes and national characteristics.

Unfortunately, the qualification *educational* would seem to imply that other forms of gymnastics are not *educational*. Rhythm is an integral part of *Educational* and women's *Olympic Gymnastics*. Yet, we do not, neither should we, draw similar implication from the name 'Rhythmical Gymnastics'. Only recently, a New Zealand teacher expressed her concern that there was 'no rhythm in Educational Gymnastics'. Names can be very misleading! They often reflect the main emphasis in content or method. It would be very difficult to find names which reflect the total scope of the work.

Perhaps, the new teaching technique was christened *educational* to denote that it was an integral part of the whole school educative process. Possibly, the initial contrast in enthusiasm for learning and consequent results were sufficient to merit such a title. Probably, it was a new label by which people might recognize a new teaching method whose main feature was extraction. Today, the new mathematical techniques would seem to be recognizable by the term 'new maths'. Simple as it seems, I would hazard a guess that the qualification 'new' has caused some resistance. Initially, new methods require open, inquiring minds. Extra effort is needed if we are to understand and so be in a position to assess relative values. Later, they need re-examination for often in our enthusiasm to embrace the new method we totally discard the old without assessing its possible contribution. The name *Educational Gymnastics* has been re-examined and it has been suggested that we replace it with the name *Movement Education*.

Whatever we call it, we must try to understand the basic concepts on which it is founded. No name, however inadequate and irritating, should prevent this. Its educational value can only be assessed when results are examined in the light of the aims inherent in the work. Furthermore, those aims must be examined in relation to the constantly changing needs of the individual or group at various stages of development.

Inglorious Isolation

Gymnastics is broken into fragments by our desire to label and separate it into categories marked 'rhythmical', 'formal' or 'educational'. We should attempt to appreciate the differences in purpose, approach and content. It is even more important to develop an understanding of the factors which unite the various categories of gymnastics. Emphases and methods may differ but results are often similar. It is possible to relate the various forms of gymnastics. It is also possible, and most valuable, to relate the integral parts of gymnastics to other movement areas, e.g. flight in gymnastics and basketball; rhythm and accent in gymnastics and the rhythm and climax of the tennis serve; gymnastic body positions and group patterns and positions and patterns which occur in synchronized swimming.

When educating through movement, an appreciation of such relationships is vital to the fuller understanding of the total scope of movement. Sensitive teachers who wish students to acquire a functional understanding and aesthetic appreciation of what the body can do, will expose them to a variety of gymnastic movement experiences and will attempt to emphasize the relationships which exist. Miss Joy Smith of the University of Otago, in an Introduction to a gymnastics course wrote:

> As teachers I feel we have an obligation to expose students to a wide repertoire of movement experiences, for some forms of movement expression are more meaningful and enjoyable to some individuals than to others. Most of us have a natural bias – swimming, hockey, formal or educational gymnastics but we must be careful not to impose our forte on others, believing it good merely because we like it.

Many of us impose our forte on young people because we enjoy it. Naturally, we might feel that we have more to offer in that particular area. Most of us do not attempt to give students an opportunity to experience the various forms of gymnastics. Of course, it is difficult, probably impossible, for an individual teacher to be all things to all people. However, if we ourselves are unable to teach a particular form of gymnastics, we could introduce it to the students through the media of films, charts, visits to competitions and demonstrations. It is to be hoped that colleges will take an increasing lead in a drive to provide a variety of gymnastic experience. Thus, newly qualified teachers would be better equipped to provide a more comprehensive gymnastic programme within the school curriculum.

It is inconceivable that teachers who can see the value of a curriculum which, at various stages, allows students to study Folk Dance, Modern Dance and Ballroom Dance cannot or will not see any merit in giving classes an opportunity to experience different gymnastic emphases. Our narrow-mindedness is reflected in the comments of both students and teachers. I have heard Educational Gymnastics fanatics say, 'I don't teach Handstands . . . we do Educational Gymnastics.' What a false impression this type of remark can create. Such comments have earned Educational Gymnastics the label 'laissez faire'.

I have heard children say, 'I can't do Gym.' Usually they are referring to specific vaults which they have been unable to achieve. For them, vaulting is gymnastics. When common sense and sensitivity to ability and current needs are applied to teaching Gymnastics, a synthesis of vaults, basic skills, rhythm, invention and discovery can be achieved. The sensitive teacher realizes that no one method can achieve such a synthesis and uses a variety of teaching methods. The method or combination of methods used will depend on the needs and interests of the individual or group concerned.

Spontaneity

Spontaneity is an outstanding feature of the Educational Gymnastics approach. The teacher carefully selects her theme and considers the scope of the tasks she intends to set the class. In this way, she can predict the *type of movements* which may evolve. However, until the students actually move in response to that stimulus, she cannot *know* the exact movements. She is often required to cope with problems and interests which arise spontaneously out of her lesson material, and adapt her teaching methods to suit the situation. Such spontaneity endows teaching with a vitality which prevents monotony and increases interest and depth of understanding for both student and teacher. Spontaneous, co-operative interchange between teacher and student is very satisfying and is of immeasurable educational value.

Educational Gymnastics is not always easy to teach. Much depends on the teacher's initiative and sensitivity. It is not easy to guide young people towards controlled independence. It is sometimes difficult to blend a variety of teaching methods to ensure that powers of invention may be developed together with a sound knowledge of skills. These same difficulties provide the challenge involved in Educational Gymnastics. When tackled with patience, common sense and above all, sensitivity to individual and group needs, the results can be very gratifying for both student and teacher.

2 Definitions of the Aims of Educational Gymnastics

In the London County Council (L.C.C.) pamphlet, handbook on Educational Gymnastics (1961), an attempt was made to differentiate the aims of the gym, dance and games lessons. The aims of the gymnastic lesson were described as follows:

> In the gymnastic lesson . . . the aim is to develop good management and control of the body and to give training in the skill needed to get over, round, along or under a variety of apparatus.[1]

This seems objective enough, especially when compared to the definition of the aims of the Dance lesson, which were defined as follows:

> The dance lesson . . . the aim is to express moods, feelings and ideas with harmonious movement. This takes the form of an artistic interpretation.[2]

The book *Teaching Gymnastics*, written by E. Mauldon and J. Layson, gives the following description of the aims of Educational Gymnastics:

> 1 To develop efficiency and a skilled use of the body in practical situations when working alone and with others, on the floor and on apparatus.
> 2 To *stimulate* an *understanding* and appreciation of objective movement coupled with the ability to invent and select appropriate actions.[3]

The second definition from *Teaching Gymnastics* states that we should aim at *understanding* objective movement. This suggests that imitative skill learning should be replaced by the student's purposeful analysis of the integral parts of movement and consideration should be given to the contribution of these parts to the whole. In a nutshell, it means that instead of being aware of WHAT the body is doing, consideration should be given to HOW the body is doing WHAT.

Example: Instead of the student knowing that she is jumping and then balancing, she will be encouraged to consciously analyse that she is jumping . . . How? . . .

Answer: By using two different types of take-offs. And balancing . . . How? . . .

Answer: On unlike parts, or on a small base with wide-shaped leg position.

3 Aims specific to Educational Gymnastics

1 To give the individual an opportunity to experience and enjoy a variety of gymnastic movements.
2 To develop specific movement skills.

---

[1] London County Council, Educational Gymnastics, unpublished handbook, 1961. This pamphlet was a prelude to the L.C.C.'s *Educational Gymnastics*, 1962. *Educational Gymnastics* is now published by the Inner London Education Authority (I.L.E.A.) previously the L.C.C.

[2] Ibid.

[3] E. Mauldon and J. Layson, *Teaching Gymnastics*, London, Macdonald and Evans, 1965, p. xii.

3 To encourage inventiveness.
4 To stimulate the *conscious* use of mind and body in the solving of gymnastic tasks.
5 To foster an understanding of the Basic Movement Factors, i.e. ability to emphasize or combine various aspects.
6 To give an opportunity for the individual to work within her own capabilities and so allow her to develop her own movement characteristics and innate abilities.
7 To provide opportunities for natural curiosity to be exercised and satisfied.

In connection with aims 4 and 7 the I.L.E.A. handbook *Educational Gymnastics* stated:

> The teacher, in presenting movement problems is appealing not only to the child's intelligence but also to her curiosity and sense of enjoyment and the child will experience great satisfaction in finding an answer to the task set.[1]

It is worth noticing that the word *an* is used and not *the*, for there are various ways of solving most movement problems.
In connection with aim 6 the Handbook stated:

> By starting with movement which the child is able to do and allowing her to continue within the limits of her own ability, she gains confidence so that she is ready and willing to attempt more difficult work.[2]

4 The Movement Factors

TIME: is concerned with the variation of speed with which movements can be done.
FLOW: is concerned with muscular control and the continuous linking of movements, through the effort of one movement carrying over to initiate the following movement.
SPACE: is concerned with the pathways, directions and levels of movement.
WEIGHT: is concerned with the actual body weight and the energy used to transfer, propel and bear that weight.

When analysing movement **four** questions arise:
What?: concerned with the WEIGHT FACTOR
How?: concerned with TIME, SPACE and FLOW FACTORS
Which?: concerned with the SPACE and WEIGHT FACTORS
Where?: concerned with the SPACE FACTOR

[1] Inner London Education Authority, op. cit., p. 4.
[2] Ibid.

5 *Major Aspects of the Factors Time, Weight, Space and Flow*

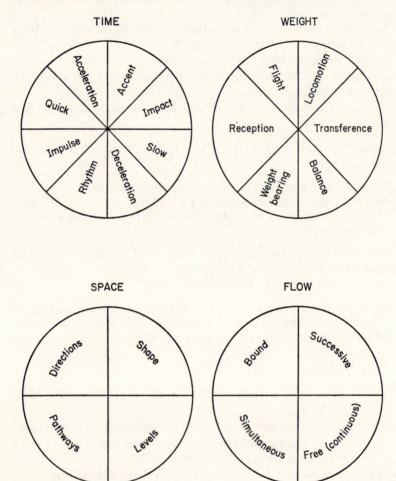

An Analysis of the Major Aspects of Space

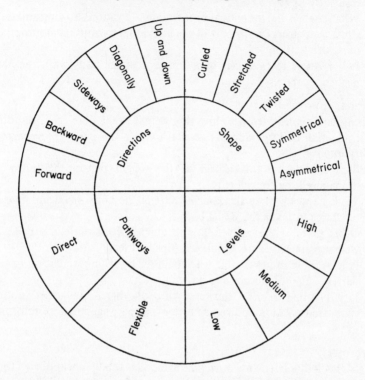

6 The Question *WHAT?* Related to the Weight Factor

Aspects of the Weight Factor are:
1 Weight Bearing
2 Reception of Weight
3 Flight
4 Transference of Weight
5 Locomotion

1 WEIGHT BEARING

The body can be supported on one or more parts. When considering what is happening to the body within this aspect of the weight factor, the following questions might arise:

Q: What is happening to the body as a whole?
A: It is being lowered or raised, stretched or curled.
Q: What happens to the body on landing from a jump?

A: The knees *give*, the seat drops low to the heels and the body recoils resiliently upwards.

Q: What enables the individual to maintain a position showing stillness?

A: Conscious effort on the part of the individual to exert the appropriate muscular tension.

Q: Is it possible to raise one or more parts of the body whilst another part supports?

2 RECEPTION OF WEIGHT

This aspect is concerned with lowering weight to the floor from standing or from small or large apparatus. *It is an essential part of introductory safety training.*

When considering this aspect of the weight factor, the following questions might be considered:

Q: What happens when the *selected* part of the body *meets the floor* in readiness to *lower* the *whole* body?

A: Other parts of the body follow in quick succession, e.g. a roll . . . weight from hands, to shoulders, hips and feet.

Q: Is it possible to lower weight to the floor by taking weight on to one part, change to another and return to feet?

Q: Is it possible to meet the floor with one part, change to another supported position and return to the first part again before returning to feet?

3 FLIGHT

Flight involves movements in which the body is totally unsupported for a short space of time. It is usually associated with height, but flight can be achieved at a low level if distance is emphasized, e.g. feet to hands to feet as in a Catspring. Emphasis is placed on the push from the feet and delayed reception of weight on to hands. Flight can be achieved off feet, hands, shoulders and a little off hips and knees when using apparatus. Working with flight means setting movement problems which ask these sorts of questions:

Q: What happens to the body in the air if insufficient muscular tension is exerted?

A: The body sags and the quality of the movement becomes heavy due to the dropping of the head and cramped position of the shoulders.

Q: What assists the body to gain height off a rope?

A: The high position of the hands, their pulling action, legs thrusting away from the rope at the *top*, i.e. maximum height of the rope swing.

Q: What sort of take-off from the feet assists in gaining distance?

A: One foot to the other.

4 TRANSFERENCE OF WEIGHT

Weight bearing is concerned with the quick shifting of weight from one part to another and can involve the holding of supported positions to show a moment of stillness.

In contrast, transference of weight is concerned with the *linking movements* which connect the supported positions.

e.g.

Held Position 1	**Linking Movement**	**Held Position 2**
. . . Handstand	. . . Backward Roll	. . . Shoulder Stand
. . . Weight Bearing	. . . Transference of Weight	. . . Weight Bearing

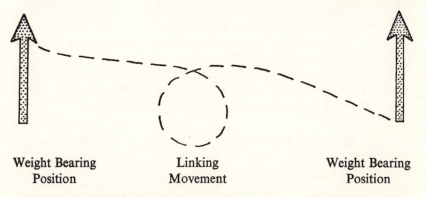

| Weight Bearing | Linking | Weight Bearing |
| Position | Movement | Position |

When working on this aspect of the weight factor set problems which raise these sorts of questions:

Q: Which movements enable us to change from one weight-bearing position to another?

A: Overbalance, rocking and rolling, etc.

Q: What assists in the use of rocking to initiate transference of weight?

A: Use of adjacent parts.

5 LOCOMOTION . . . i.e. **Travelling**

There are various ways of travelling which will be considered later. In considering the question **What?** the following type of question might arise from tasks set to produce locomotion:

Q: What happens when using hands and feet to travel?

A: Feet chase hands. Feet overtake hands.

When considering the weight factor, it is not sufficient merely to emphasize what is happening to the actual body weight as outlined above. It is also necessary to work towards an awareness concerning the degree of muscular tension which must be used in the various movement situations.

Muscular tension can be **heavy, light** or **strong,** and the degree of tension used is constantly changing. It is important to emphasize suitable use of muscular tension.

Heavy degree of tension involves the controlled release of tension, i.e. relaxation, and is necessary to safety in the recovery phase of any movement, e.g. *give* of the knees, possibly a roll in landing from height before returning to normal standing position. It assists sensitive lowering of the body weight, i.e. reception of weight, and can often be used to initiate linking movements, i.e. transference of weight.

Light degree of tension provides softness in travelling and a resilience when raising the body from the floor or apparatus. It also provides an impression of easily maintained poise in flight and well-held position in weight-bearing. Such poise and precise positioning arise from the conscious, *sustained* application of muscular tension. Such tension should be encouraged in locomotion and flight.

Strong tension involves the sudden, almost explosive, exertion of muscular power, e.g. accelerating run, strong double take-off to propel the body into a position with the hands high on two ropes.

7   The Question *HOW?* Applied to Aspects of Time and Space

(i)   How quickly or slowly can the body move?
(Time factor)
(ii) How many directions can the body use?
(Space factor)
(iii) How many levels are used?
(Space factor)
(iv) How can we gather impetus to clear a high box?
(Time factor)
Answer: Through acceleration.
(v)   How do we achieve continuity of movement?
Answer: By anticipation of the next movement and positioning of the weight-bearing parts in such a way that transition is made easier.
Example: A Forward Roll into a Handstand in which feet are placed one in front of the other to facilitate transition into the Handstand.

8   The Question *WHICH?* Applied to Space and Weight Factors

When working on various aspects of the movement factors weight, space and flow it can be valuable to set tasks which prompt the following type of questions:

(i) **Which** part of the body is receiving weight first?
   Which part follows?
(ii) **Which** part of the body is supporting?
(iii) **Which** part is being lifted high?
(iv) **Which** take-off would be suitable to negotiate a wide space between
   two pieces of apparatus?
(v) **Which** part initiated the transference of weight?
(vi) **Which** part initiated the change of level or direction?
(vii) **Which** direction did the sequence emphasize?

9   The Question *WHERE?* Applied to Aspects of Space

This question is concerned with the use of the body in both *personal* and
general space.
Examples:
Q: Where is the body going?
A: Upwards . . . downwards . . . forwards.
Q: Where does the movement occur?
A: In the personal space, e.g. knee arabesque.
   In the general space, e.g. travelling using cartwheels from one place
   in the gym to another.
   Tasks and the questions they raise must always be answered in **Move-
ment**, i.e. by pupils moving themselves and possibly through observing
movement in others.

10 Apparatus . . . Identification

Bench – broad side up

Bench – balance side up

Bench – hooked on to apparatus

Box horse – (number indicates the
   number of layers)

Horse without pommels

Horse with 1 pommel

Horse with 2 pommels

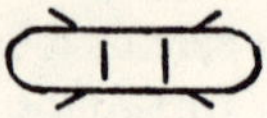

Vaulting Stool (Vaulting Buck)

Mini-tramp

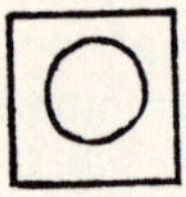

Beat board (Springboard)

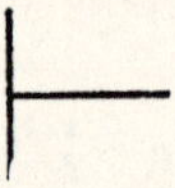

Mat

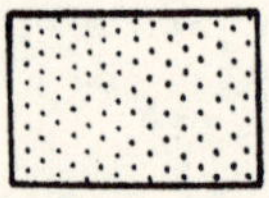

Long mat

Olympic Beam (Balance beam, balance rail)

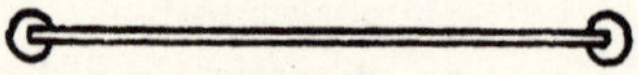

Swedish Beam

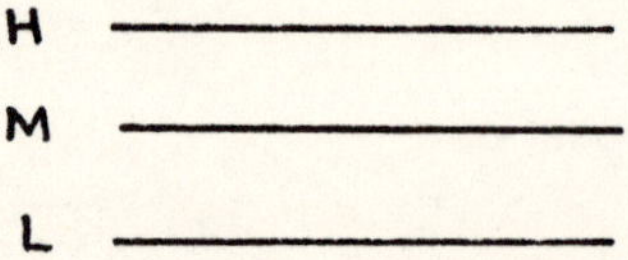

H ————————— High

M ————————— Medium

L ————————— Low

b s u = balance side up

Ropes

Wall Bars

Window Ladder Frame (Cave Southampton)

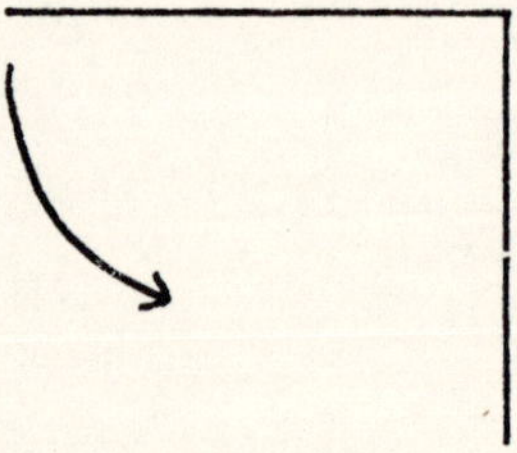

PART TWO: Shaping the Lesson

1 Mechanics of the Lesson

Part 1: Limbering (Warm-up)
> Duration: 3–4 minutes only.

Purposes

1 To prepare the class both mentally and physically for work to follow.
2 To give an opportunity to remember and practise skills and movement ideas.

Provide specific tasks. Don't say 'Practise anything you like!'

Task Examples

  (i) Practise a Handstand lowering into a Forward Roll.
 (ii) Run – jump – roll and spring up. Keep repeating.
(iii) Try to remember some of your previous ideas on curling and stretching – try to link them and make a continuous sequence.
(iv) Make a sequence showing stretched, curled and twisted shapes. Keep repeating.

Part 2: Movement Training
> Duration: **variable,** i.e. can take up one-third, a half or two-thirds of the lesson according to newness of the theme.

Purpose: The Movement Theme is introduced or developed.

Task Examples

Theme: **Balance**
Is it possible to balance on unlike parts of the body?

Theme: **Levels,** an Aspect of Space
Can you travel across the floor at two different levels?
> *or*

Travel showing movements at high and low levels.

Theme: **Locomotion on Hands**
Find ways of travelling on hands.
> *or*

Can you use hands to travel showing movements in which the feet overtake the hands?

Theme: **Direction,** an Aspect of Space.
How many directions can we use in moving about the gym?
> *or*

Move in forwards, sideways and backwards direction.

In this part of the lesson the theme is explored or further developed. Individuals are encouraged to invent sequences of movement which suit the lesson theme.

When the new idea has been explored, this part of the lesson may consequently be used to repeat newly discovered skills. Partner or group work might be introduced as an extension within the selected theme.

Sequences can be developed under the headings:

A. Whole body
B. Weight supported on arms
C. Leg work

and/or combinations:

A, B and C; A and B; B and C; A and C.[1]

Small apparatus such as benches and mats can be used preparatory to large apparatus.

Part 3: Apparatus

This is the climax of the lesson. Duration will vary correspondingly with the Movement Training section.

The theme introduced or developed in the Movement Training section is carried over to the Apparatus section. **Sometimes** movements discovered and practised on the floor or on small apparatus within the Movement Training may be **literally** transferred to larger apparatus.

Example

An individual having used a Handstand followed by a Bunny Hop in Movement Training, might use these two movements and transfer them literally to the following apparatus.

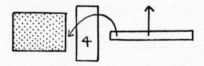

or

A **Movement Idea** may be transferred to apparatus.

Example

Task in Movement Training: Take weight from feet to hands back to feet.

Movement Used: A Handstand . . . which is an inverted position with weight on hands.

Transferred to Two Ropes: Inverted position . . . feet above head, body stretched, hands pulling on the rope to support the body.

[1] Ibid., p. 9.

Literal transference of movements may not be possible on the apparatus, but it is **always** possible to transfer the **movement idea**. The theme is considered in connection with arriving on, departing from, going over, round, through and under apparatus.

Flexibility of Timing
Time the sections on Movement Training and Apparatus according to the progress and interest of the group. It is very likely that in the introductory stages group members will need more time on movement training so that they may discover and **repeat** new skills at their own pace.

When introducing partner and group extension to a theme you might even spend *two-thirds* of the first lesson on movement training. If this is the case, consider using the remainder of the lesson for small apparatus work. The following lesson you might begin after limbering on small apparatus and progress at half-time to large apparatus. If the group is interested or needs extra practice do not worry if you spend the *whole introductory* lesson on movement training. Similarly you may decide to use small apparatus for the whole of the following lesson.

2 Stages of Learning

In Educational Gymnastics there are three main stages of learning:

1 Exploration
2 Repetition
3 Selection

1 Exploration: This is the stage at which an individual is allowed freedom to discover answers to movement tasks and to invent movement sequences suitable to the theme. It is a trial and error stage. At this stage, you must be sensitive to the individual needs within the group. Some individuals will be pleased to receive your movement suggestions. Others will prefer to be left alone with the problem.

Having satisfied their independence and curiosity they might ask, 'Is this all right?' Observe carefully in the initial stages. When an individual hesitates, *then* step in and make suggestions aimed at improving general points such as well-held, clearly-defined body shape or continuity of movement. When continuity is poor, suggest suitable rearrangement of movements within the sequence.

2 Repetition: During this stage newly discovered skills and invented sequences are repeated. Repetition of sequences is a valuable process because:
(a) It helps the individual to memorize skills and sequence patterns.
(b) Fluency of movement can be perfected.

(c) It gives the individual an opportunity to raise her own standard.

(d) It affords the teacher an opportunity to observe the standard and progress of the group.

This is a good time at which to introduce any Partner Work which involves *copying* movements. Partner Work gives the individual an opportunity to pass on her carefully worked out and memorized sequence and to have the satisfaction of sharing her movement ideas. By copying her partner's sequence an individual can learn to appreciate the variety of ways in which movement problems may be solved.

3 Selection: Following Exploration and Repetition there arrives a stage of Selection. In exploring answers to movement problems and repeating skills and invented sequences, the individual acquires a '*movement vocabulary*'. As she progresses from theme to theme and her vocabulary grows, so she is able to select from her increasing repertoire, skills and movement ideas which will suitably answer new tasks.

Teachers often spend time at exploring but often neglect to allow sufficient time for ideas and skills to be consolidated through repetition. Allow time for repetition so that the group may enjoy the new skills.

3   Methods of Teaching in Educational Gymnastics

The better teacher uses a variety of teaching methods either separately or in conjunction with each other. There are three main types of teaching methods:

1 Direct
2 Indirect
3 Limitation

1 Direct Method: This method is completely teacher dominated and the individual has no choice of activity or apparatus.

Example Tasks
 (i) Practise a Handstand followed by a Forward Roll.
(ii) Practise a Backward Roll lifting upwards into a Handstand.
On small apparatus
 (i) Arrive on the bench with a Forward Roll and jump off the end using a double take-off.
(ii) Jump on to the bench, lower your weight, go into a Shoulder Stand position, back to feet and jump off the end of the bench.
On large apparatus
 (i) Arrive with two feet on the box, roll along it and jump off the end using a single take-off.

(ii) Swing from the rope to land with two feet together on the beam, jump off and show a stretched position in the air.

The individual has no choice either in the use of body parts or in the use of apparatus. Individuals will sometimes decide, 'I can't do that' or will be satisfied with producing the same movements for most themes. If this is so, use the **Direct Method** of teaching to increase their *movement vocabulary*. This method of teaching increases the challenge, produces a variety of skills and prevents the repetitive use of any one particular movement or pattern of movements.

2 Indirect Method: This method is concerned with extracting ideas and movements from the group rather than *pouring in*. It encourages the group to explore the movement possibilities within any selected theme.

Example Tasks
  (i) How many different shapes can you show in moving about the gym?
 (ii) How many different directions can you use?
(iii) Is it possible to travel using your hands?
(iv) Is it possible to make *gestures* with legs whilst weight is supported on another part of the body?
On small apparatus
  (i) Find different ways of going across the mat.
 (ii) Find ways of moving along and over the bench.
On large apparatus
  (i) Find ways of getting on and off the box.
 (ii) On the Swedish beam . . . find different ways of getting on, travelling along, over and off the beam.
(iii) On the Olympic beam . . . is it possible to change leg shapes whilst weight is on other parts of the body?
(iv) Use two ropes in a variety of ways.

By allowing exploration, this method usually produces variety of movement ideas. You should have considered the possible scope of movements so that *you* may make *suggestions* to help the less inventive or less able.

3 Limitation Method: This method is a mixture of Direct and Indirect Methods because the individual is allowed choice but within the limitations set by the teacher.

Example Tasks
  (i) *Using the floor:* Take your weight on to your hands and lift your feet off the floor.
      Possible actions are: Handstand, Catspring, Bunny Hop, Headspring, Cartwheel, etc.

The class is **limited** to the **use of hands** but within that limitation they have freedom of choice of movements.
(ii) Travel in a forwards, sideways and backwards direction.

Many movements can be found to answer this movement problem and each individual is free to choose which movements she will use within the limitation of forwards, sideways and backwards directions. Such tasks can be extended to use on small and larger apparatus.

Limitation can be achieved by:
  (i) Stipulating which *area* or *specific part* of the body is to be used.
 (ii) Stipulating *pathway* . . . e.g. over and under or over and through or through, under and through again.
(iii) Stipulating at which *level* or in which *direction* movement is to occur.
(iv) Stipulating *definite sequence* of use on the apparatus, e.g. Use the bench, mat and bench again, or use the box, rope, box and rope again.

Movement and Action Tasks
When tasks are set which *allow freedom of choice* these are **Movement Tasks.** When tasks are set which *restrict* the individual as indicated above, these are **Action Tasks.** Apparatus sections may be:
  (i) All Movement Task sections.
 (ii) All Action Task sections.
(iii) Half Action and half Movement Tasks.
(iv) One or two Action Tasks, the remaining sections Movement Tasks.
 (v) One or two Movement Tasks, the remaining sections Action Tasks.

When first introducing a theme you will *probably* use the Indirect Method and so apparatus will be set with Movement Tasks.

Whilst it is true that the theme itself should be sufficiently challenging, the Action Task, with its teacher-imposed limitations does provide a more clearly defined and more easily recognizable challenge.

Following the introductory stage of the theme, consider using a mixture of Movement and Action Tasks to present a dual challenge of inventiveness and the use of skill within limitations.

4   Observation

1 Position yourself so that you may alternately watch the whole class and move about to help individuals.
2 Watch to see whether the class is fulfilling the task set and help individuals who might be having difficulty.
3 Observe whether real demands have been made on the group.

4 Watch for individual, partner and group work which may be useful in the illustration of a point which you have decided to emphasize.

5 Observe progress made and interest shown and make a note on your lesson plans of possible progressions and what you consider the suitable ratio of Movement Training and Apparatus sections to be for subsequent lessons.

6 Do **not** observe for the sake of observing.

7 Give the group a definite point to watch or ask them a question, the answer to which will come from their observation, e.g.:

  (i) Use of space within the group.
  (ii) Variety of levels used . . . which?
  (iii) Awareness of change of speed *or* rhythm, *or* well held balance positions *or* a variety of ways of transferring weight from position to position

or

Ask questions such as:

  (i) What sort of take-off did she use? *Why?*
  (ii) What shapes did the body assume in using the pathway over-under-through on the double Swedish beam?

8 When observing, you might ask one half of the group using sections along one side of the gym, to watch the other half. If you wish to show two sections at once for observation of a point such as spacing within the group, or variety of levels, choose *adjacent* groups to make observation easier both for you and the class.

9 Do not expect a group to be able to observe several scattered individual performances. If you wish to show individuals working, show six or eight only and bring them into the centre of the gym so that all can see.

10 Try not to choose the most capable all the time. However simple a movement appears to be, use it if it illustrates your point.

11 When the demonstration(s) is(are) completed **do not** say 'Good'. If it is good . . . **say why,** or ask the group, 'Why is this so satisfying to watch?'

  If the sequence is not as good as it might be, **do not** say 'That is coming', but without being publicly destructive, offer constructive general suggestions, e.g.

  (i) 'Perhaps you could emphasize the body shape a little more . . .'
  (ii) 'Your ideas were good, but your movements lacked *finish*. Now, if you were to stretch a little further and do every movement to its full extent . . .'
  (iii) 'I liked this idea, but would a change of speed improve the sequence?'

5 General Points

Throughout all themes, emphasize the following points:
1 Clearly defined starting and finishing positions in both floor and apparatus work.
2 Continuity of movement.
3 Performance of all movements to their full extent, i.e. clearly defined body shape and position both during flight and when supported.
4 Toes to be extended, head lifted in flight.
5 Constant activity within the group both working on the floor and on apparatus.
6 Resilience in *recovery* from the floor and from apparatus.
7 Spacing: Avoiding others within the group by starting individual sequences from different places within the section.
8 Care in lifting and lowering apparatus.
9 Efficient co-operation in arranging and clearing apparatus.
10 Once movements have been discovered or selected encourage the class members to **perfect** their sequences.

PART THREE: Lesson content

Themes, Progressions and Extensions

SECTION 1 **Basic Body Management**
Stage 1: Preliminary Footwork, Flight and Weight Reception
1 Preliminary Footwork.
2 Basic Flight.
3 Reception of Weight.
4 Combination of 2 and 3.
Stage 2: Weight Bearing
1 Lowering weight on to different parts of the body.
2 Raising parts of the body.
3 Emphasizing Stillness.
4 Weight on Hands.
Stage 3: Transference of Weight[1]
1 Rocking and rolling.
2 Flight.
3 Step-like actions.
Stage 4: Combination of Basic Flight, Weight Bearing and Transference of Weight
Stage 5: Locomotion or Travelling

SECTION 2
Further Progressions
1 Body Shape.
2 Balance.
3 Emphasis on aspects of the Space factor.
4 Emphasis on aspects of the Time factor.
5 Emphasis on aspects of the Flow factor.
6 Combining aspects of the Movement factors.

SECTION 3
Advanced Work
1 Combinations of Themes.
2 Assessment of the Relationships between Movement Themes.
3 Losing and Regaining Balance.
4 Flight.

SECTION 4
Extensions
1 Partner Work.
2 Group Work.

[1] Mauldon and Layson, op. cit., pp. 46–48.

SECTION 5
College Workshops

SECTION 1: Basic Body Management

STAGE 1: Preliminary Footwork, Flight and Weight Reception

Primary Aims: Safety.
Confidence.
Sensitivity of feet.
Resilience in *recovery*.

1 Preliminary Footwork
It is essential for the class to discover and practise ways of using the feet efficiently and sensitively.

Possible Activities
   (i) Running on toes, walking on heels, running on toes.
  (ii) Long striding getting a strong push from the back leg.
 (iii) Jumping on the spot, with alternate 'give' and stretch of the ankles.
 (iv) Combinations: (i) and (ii); (ii) and (iii); (i), (ii) and (iii).
  (v) Making floor patterns on the spot with feet, e.g. square, circle – using small steps.
 (vi) Making floor patterns travelling in the General Space.
(vii) Skipping with or without ropes.
(viii) Combinations of (v) and (vi).

2 Basic Flight
Methods of Taking off and Landing
  (i) From two feet to two feet (2–2).
 (ii) From one foot to two feet (1–2).
(iii) From two feet to one foot (2–1).
 (iv) From one foot to the other (1–Other).
  (v) From one foot to the same (1–1).

Methods
Indirect (Complete extraction) e.g.:
There are five possible ways of using the feet to take off and land. See if you can find them.
How many ways can you use your feet to take off and land?

Direct followed by Indirect e.g.:
Try to jump from one foot to the other and make the stride as wide as you can. Get a good push off from the back leg. (Direct.)
followed by
Can you find another way of taking off and landing? (Indirect.)

Direct, Indirect, Direct
The teacher gives one method, the group finds another, the teacher gives another.

The use of direct or indirect methods will depend on the group's willingness to try out ideas for themselves. If they hesitate, use direct method and extend to indirect as confidence grows so that they become more independent. (When referring to indirect, direct and limitation teaching methods the letters I, D and L will be used.)

What next?
(i) Construct a sequence of jumps which is short and easily repeated.
(ii) Consider which jumps afford height or distance or both, e.g.:

1–1   – little height or distance.

1–Other – gives height and distance.

2–2   – gives a fair amount of height in the personal space. Little possibility of distance except when used in conjunction with swinging ropes, Swedish beam or bars.

Use of Apparatus
Small Apparatus: Use small apparatus in the initial stages, e.g. benches, mats, box tops. Arrangement of apparatus may be formal or free.
Examples of Formal and Free Apparatus Arrangements

(I) = Indirect   (D) = Direct   (L) = Limited

Formal
1 *Tasks on benches*
(i) Run along bench, jump from two feet to two feet. (D)
(ii) Zig-zag jumping over the bench using take-offs, 2–2, 1–2, 2–1. (D)

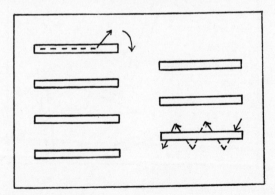

2 *Tasks on benches and mats*
Travelling from one end of the bench to the other,
(i) Show three different take-offs and landings. (L)

(ii) Show a variety of take-offs and landings to cross over to the opposite
     side of the mat. (L)
     Use corners and choose jumps suitable for the distance to be crossed.

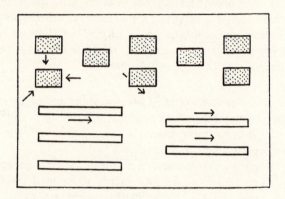

Informal

Tasks on benches

(i) Using any type of take-off and landing travel anywhere in the gym,
    jumping on, off, over and along the benches. (I)
(ii) Travel anywhere using a combination of take-offs, e.g. one foot to
     the other, two feet to two feet. (L)
(iii) (*a*) Jump over benches using one foot to the other. (D)
      (*b*) Land on benches with two feet and jump off to land on the floor
            with two feet. (D)

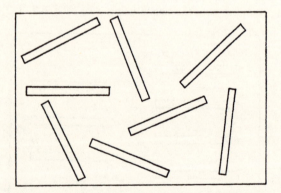

Tasks on benches and mats

(i) Show 'distance' jumps to clear the mats. (L)
(ii) Travel along the benches using one foot to two feet, two feet to two
     feet and two feet to one foot. (D)

(iii) Combination of (i) and (ii).

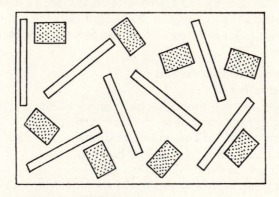

The Group Working in Two Halves
One half . . . Travelling anywhere non-stop using benches only; use any of the five take-offs and landings. (L)
The other half . . . Using all the mats. Show non-stop sequence of all types of take-offs and landings. (L)

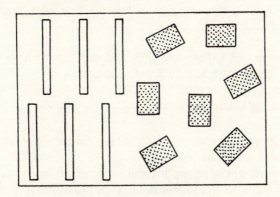

The only limitation is the type of apparatus used, otherwise the group has complete freedom of pathways and actual construction of sequence.

Tasks may be Indirect, Direct or Limited in both formal and informal arrangements of apparatus.

Possible Combinations of Tasks
   (i) Freedom in Space . . . Set take-offs and landings, i.e. one foot to the other, two feet to two feet. (L)
  (ii) Restricted use of Space (using one bench or one mat) using any type of take-off and landing. (L)

(iii) Freedom to go anywhere using any take-offs and landings. (I)
(iv) Restricted in Space and definite take-off and landing to be used. (D)
(v) Restricted in Space using teacher-defined sequence, e.g. one foot to the other followed by two feet to one foot followed by two feet to two feet. (D)

Developing Sensitivity of the Feet

Swedish Beam (b s u)
(i) Walking on toes – forwards – backwards – sideways.
(ii) Springing from one foot to the other; turning.
(iii) Lowering weight to hips, to one knee, returning to standing.
(iv) Arabesques – rolls, forwards and backwards.
(v) Jumping on to and off the beam.

Encourage placing of toes and *feeling* the beam with soles of the feet.

Ropes
(i) Climbing rope, emphasizing pull of arms and *gripping* with feet.
(ii) Swinging – *gathering* the rope with hands to gain impetus for high swing, thrusting legs away from rope at the top of its swing – landing with two feet on mat or into a hoop.

Emphasize push of feet from the floor in single and double take-off and controlled landing showing *give* in knees and recoil *upwards* to good standing position.

Large Apparatus
Extend the use of various take-offs and landings to large apparatus.
Gradually increase the height and/or distances.

Aims
(i) To present combinations of apparatus which suggest a variety of approaches.
(ii) To augment an understanding of the theme within the objective apparatus situations.

The arrangement of apparatus will be governed by the theme of the lesson and the tasks set. Tasks can be set in two different ways:

All groups have the same task but work at different pieces of apparatus, e.g. Travel over, round and through the apparatus showing variety of take-offs and landings.

A different task is given to each group, e.g.:
(i) Travel over box, bench and mat showing two feet to two feet take-offs and landings. (L)
(ii) Show three different types of take-offs within your section. (I)
(iii) Placing hands on the top beam jump from two feet through a double Swedish beam to land on two feet and use the landing as take-off to go over the adjacent box. (L)

You **must plan** your apparatus and suit its arrangement to the theme you have selected.

Encourage use of surrounding floor space and **keep the group moving.**

If only one pathway is suggested in the formally set apparatus section and the directed activity, e.g. weight on hands and flight, necessitates a longer approach to facilitate acceleration, encourage the remainder of the group within that section to practise movements in the surrounding space. Alternatively, provide a practice bench or mat at the side of the section, e.g. Handstand, Headspring practice could be done individually or with partner assistance.

A variety of possible approaches will keep your group moving and also suggest different types of take-offs and landings according to height and distances to be negotiated.

Example:

 (i) Two pommels suggest the use of two hands. One pommel might suggest uneven use of hands or even the use of one hand only.

(ii) A mat set straight at the end of the box might suggest two feet to two feet take-off from box to floor if mat is close to the box.

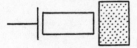

Increase distance

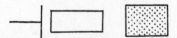

and possibly one foot to the other take-off will result.

(iii) A bar or single Swedish beam above head height with the task:
    Jump and get on to the bar using hands
will possibly produce double take-offs.

A bar or single Swedish beam at waist height with the task:
    Jump over the bar without touching it with hands or feet
will, in all probability, produce one foot to the other, or one foot take-off to land on two feet.

COMBINATIONS OF APPARATUS

Examples of Freely Arranged Apparatus

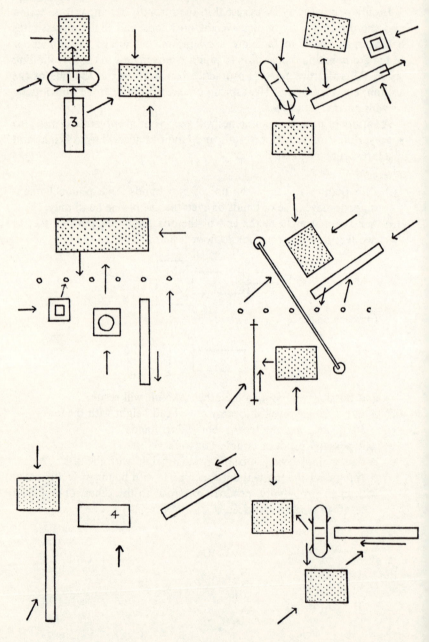

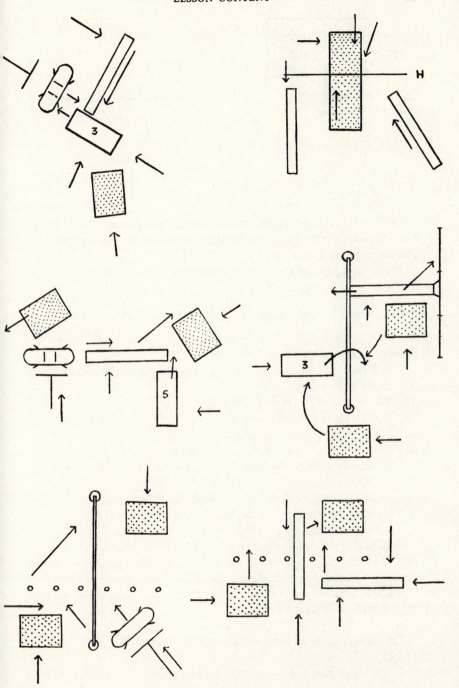

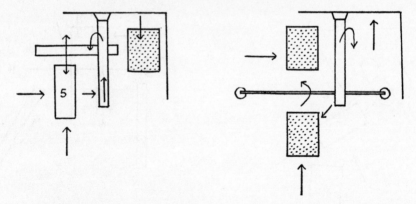

Often teachers are limited due to lack of equipment. If this is the case, consider combining one section freely and set the remainder of the apparatus in the formal way.

These examples are to illustrate the possible variety of combinations and approach on apparatus.

3 Reception of Weight – Lowering and Raising the Body

Methods
Indirect – exploratory stage. Consider:
  (i) Is it possible to lower your whole body weight slowly and carefully to the floor and return to your feet?
 (ii) Which part of the body is meeting the floor first?
(iii) Is it possible for another part of the body to arrive on the floor first?
 (iv) Can you find another way back to the feet?
      e.g. hands meeting the floor first . . . weight to hips, knees and feet
                              or
      hands meeting the floor first . . . Forward Roll back to feet.
  (v) Can you roll on meeting the floor? How many ways? e.g. forwards, backwards, sideways.

Pose such questions to the group members and invite them to explore and discover various answers **in movement.** You might **prompt** whilst the group is working with such phrases as:

If you have taken your weight on your knees first . . . see if you can now take weight on to hands first.

                              or

Try taking weight on to one part, changing to another before returning to feet.

Think which part is going to receive weight next.

Direct

Task

(i) Slowly lower your weight to allow your knees to meet the floor first, roll on to hips, over to one knee, and back to feet. Repeat.

Limited

Tasks

(i) Lower your weight to the floor and receive your weight first on a part of the body which is above the level of the waist and secondly on a part below waist level.

(ii) Lower your weight. Receive weight on a part on the right side of the body, followed by a part on the left-hand side. Return to feet.

These ideas can be extended for use on small and large apparatus.

Apparatus

When extending the theme *Reception of Weight* to apparatus consider how to:

(i) Lower weight from a low piece of apparatus to the floor.

(ii) Negotiate spaces between pieces of apparatus of (approximalety) *equal* height.

(iii) Negotiate spaces between pieces of apparatus of *unequal* height.

It is essential to use low apparatus in the introductory stages.

On the apparatus illustrated below, it would be possible to lower weight from bench to floor, i.e. (i), negotiate the space between pommel horse and box, i.e. (ii), and receive weight from pommel horse to bench, i.e. (iii).

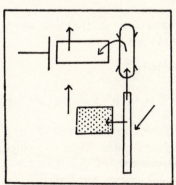

4 Combination of Basic Flight and Reception of Weight

Work at sequences to show:

(i) Jump – roll – jump.

(ii) Jump – lower the body, change weight, change again, jump up.

Extend to benches and mats and large apparatus. Use any of the three teaching methods.

STAGE 2: **Weight Bearing**

1 Lowering weight on to different parts of the body
Encourage the use of different parts meeting the floor first, e.g. hips – hands – shoulders.

Methods

Direct
Slowly lower your weight to allow your knees to meet the floor first, roll on to hips, over to one knee and return to feet.

Indirect
  (i) Can you lower your weight to the floor and return to your feet?
then
 (ii) Can you let another part meet the floor first this time . . . return to feet?
or
(iii) Can you lower your weight, meeting the floor with one part, change weight to another part and return to feet.
then
(iv) Can you lower your weight and continue to shift weight allowing **several** parts to support you in turn?

Limited
Meet the floor with hands first . . . lower your weight, change to any other body part and return to feet.

2 Raising parts of the body
Possible Tasks
  (i) Lift *one part high*, come down, change the support and lift the *same part high* again.
 (ii) Lift *one part*, different support, a *second part* high.
(iii) Lift *one part* high and lower weight on to that *same part*.
(iv) Choose starting position, lift one part high. Return to the *same starting position*, lift *another part high*.

3 Emphasizing Stillness
This involves supporting the body on different parts and *holding a position* whilst supported. Emphasize awareness of *muscular tension* needed to hold a definite position.

Possible Tasks
 (i) Take weight on part of the body – hold a definite position to show
     clearly which part is supporting the body.
(ii) Take weight on to hands, change and support the body on two
     shoulders – hold the position – return to feet.

4 Weight on Hands

Methods

Direct
Using Personal Space
Place both hands on the floor, keep them there and try to lift the body off
the floor.

   Emphasize *placing* the hands and lifting the head, pushing out the
chin in the inverted position. Tipping over can be avoided by half
turning at the hips in the inverted position, so that feet land to the side of
the original starting position.

Limited
Using General Space
Allow the group to attempt any one or all of the following methods of
taking weight on hands:
  (i) One foot to two hands, landing on one or two feet.
 (ii) From two feet to two hands, landing on one or two feet.
(iii) From one foot to one hand, landing on two or one foot.
(iv) From one foot to one hand to the other hand, landing on one or two
     feet.
 (v) From two feet to one hand to the other hand, landing on one or two
     feet.[1]
These ideas can be transferred to large apparatus.

Indirect
(*a*) *Using Personal Space*

Example Tasks
  (i) Can you take weight from feet to hands and back to feet again?
 (ii) Is it possible to take weight from one foot to two hands, achieve
      an inverted position and use the second foot to return to the floor?
(iii) Can you take off on two feet, take weight on hands, release one hand
      and return to feet?
(*b*) *Using the General Space*

[1] I.L.E.A. op. cit., p. 28.

Example Tasks
  (i) How many different ways can you take off from feet and use hands to bear your weight?
 (ii) Is it possible to have a single take-off (i.e. off one foot) take weight from one hand to the other hand and return to feet?
(iii) Take weight from feet to hands and back to feet. Try to travel a long way from your starting position.

Using mats only
Examples:

Direct
  (i) Use a double take-off (i.e. two feet) to go into a Handstand.
 (ii) Use a single take-off to go into a Handstand.
(iii) Hands to be placed in the centre of the mat, bring legs high over the top to land on the opposite side of the mat, i.e. Cartwheel or Round-off, possibly a Handspring.
(iv) Handspring practice.

Indirect
Take weight from feet to hands to feet. How many movements can you find?

Limited
Find ways of taking weight from two feet to two hands to two feet.

Using Small Apparatus
A *General Task* may be set, e.g.:
Wherever you are working, use a take-off from two feet, to take weight on two hands and return to feet.

or

Several different tasks may be set, i.e. a different task at each section.
Examples:
General Tasks on this formally set apparatus shown below might be:
  (i) Take weight from two feet to two hands to two feet using the bench and mat. (L)
Possible Movements: Catspring, Bunny hop, Handspring, Handstand, or Handstand with a half or quarter turn.
 (ii) Find two ways of taking off from feet and using hands on benches and mats. (L)

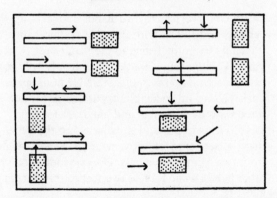

Everyone is working on similarly set apparatus on *one type* of task which may be indirect, direct or limited in approach.

N.B. Arrows indicate a variety of approaches. Four bench and mat arrangements are shown here. The arrangement *can* be completely uniform.

Examples – Tasks for freely set apparatus

Tasks may be general, e.g. whichever section you are on, show a sequence using feet-hands-feet-hands-feet.

or

Tasks may be *varied*, a different task being set at each section.

Examples:

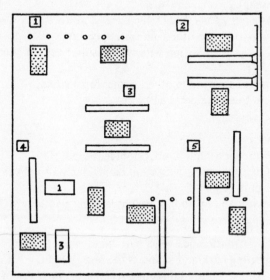

Section 1 – Task: Show sequence from two feet to two hands to two feet (1) on the rope and (2) on the mat. (L)

Section 2 – Task: Use two feet to two hands to travel up the inclined benches and follow with one foot to two hands to two feet travelling from the bench to the mat. (L)

Section 3 – Task: Taking weight from feet to hands *keep moving* using two benches, two mats and available floor space. (L)

Section 4 – Task: Using all available apparatus and floor space, find three ways of using feet and hands. (L)

Section 5 – Task: Using ropes and moving along the bench, i.e. *on* it, show a sequence of movement in which weight is taken from two feet to two hands. Use one foot to one hand to the other hand to one foot or two feet to travel from benches to mats. (L)

An alternative task for section 4 might be: Move from place to place within the section, using all the apparatus without touching the floor, taking weight from feet to hands to feet.

STAGE 3: **Transference of Weight** (Linking positions of Stillness)
Types of Linking movements:
1 Rocking and rolling
2 Flight, i.e. jumping
3 Step-like actions

1 Rocking and Rolling
Example Tasks
(i) *Find two parts of the body* which are close to each other and rock from one part to the other. *Increase speed* and *gathering momentum*, roll and take up a position with weight supported on another part of the body. (L)
(ii) Rock from one part to another, gather momentum, roll and continue to rock on the same parts. (L)

2 Flight
Example Tasks
(i) Show Shoulder Stand, jump, Shoulder Stand. (D)
(ii) Construct a sequence: weight on hands, jump, weight supported on another part. (L)
(iii) Can you use a jump to link weight bearing positions? (I)

3 Step-like Actions
In this type of transference, one part takes weight, another *overtakes* the first supporting part, and supports the body weight, e.g. Cartwheel.
(i) Encourage use of non-adjacent parts, particularly use of hands and feet.
(ii) Refer to Stage 2 (4) *Weight on Hands*.

(iii) Use on small or large apparatus.

(iv) Encourage separate and combined use of methods of transferring weight, e.g. show a sequence taking weight on different parts of the body linking weight bearing positions in a variety of ways, or in two different ways.

STAGE 4: **Combination of Basic Flight, Weight Bearing and Transference of Weight**

Examples:

(i) Jump, take weight on three different parts of the body in quick succession, and choose your own method of linking the movement positions. (L)

(ii) Take your weight on one particular part of the body, rock and roll out and back into that position. (L)

(iii) Jump, land and take weight on to shoulders, to feet to hands, to feet to hands, shoulders to feet . . . Use rock and roll method of transferring weight and linking positions. (D)

(iv) Using any part of the body and any take-off, show a sequence using different parts of the body to bear weight and show two ways of linking these movements. (I)

STAGE 5: **Travelling or Locomotion**

Methods of travelling at floor level are:

1 Using feet only. (Refer to Basic Flight Section.)

2 Using hands and feet. (Refer to Stage 3 (3).)

(*a*) Hands can be chased by feet

or

(*b*) Feet can overtake hands.

3 Rolling: Emphasize variety in exploratory stages. Also stress compactness of the curled roll and the *long line* of the stretched roll.

4 Using hands only . . . This is advanced floor work.[1]

Methods of Travelling on Apparatus:

In addition to 1, 2 and 3 as outlined above there are two methods:

1 Gripping and releasing.

2 *Using hands only* – as when using Swedish beam, ropes and window ladder frames.[2]

1 *Gripping and Releasing*

Encourage your group to grip using different parts of the feet, back of the knees, front of the hips and to show alternate use of hands and feet.

---

[1] Mauldon and Layson, op. cit., p. 34.
[2] Ibid. pp. 35–36.

You might use single and/or double Swedish beam and bars, ropes, pommel horse, window ladder frames, or wall bars.

Examples: Task on Ropes

Climbing a single rope, push with the feet and pull with the arms alternately until you reach the top of the rope. (L)

Task on single Swedish beam or bar

Sideways travelling *alternately lifting hands* to travel from one side to the other. (L)

Task on double Swedish beam

Take off from two feet, arrive with two hands on the top beam, lift knees, stretch legs through the space between the beams, release the hand grip and land on the opposite side. (D) (Heave Vault.)

2 *Locomotion Using Hands*

When using the floor emphasize distance. Consider the value of providing obstacles such as benches and box tops. If you decide to use obstacles to help the group achieve distance, set such tasks as:

  (i) Stand at one side of the bench. Place hands on the bench and push to raise hips and feet high over the hands to land as far away as possible from the bench. (L)

 (ii) Start with one hand on the bench and land on the other side with two feet. (L)

(iii) Travel from one end of the bench to the other, moving from floor to bench to floor, and show feet chasing hands or feet overtaking hands. (L)

In observation, you could ask the group to *identify* which method of *travelling on hands* the demonstrator used.

Progression

Once the group has discovered ways of travelling try to develop ability to **arrest movement** within the *Travelling Sequence*.

SELECTION IN TEACHING STAGES

It is **NOT NECESSARY** to follow the teaching pattern of Stage 1 through to Stage 5 in numerical order as here indicated.

Order **could** be: Stages 1 : 2 : 5 : 3 : 4
Stages 1 : 5 : 3 : 2 : 4
Stages 1 : 2 : 3 : 4 : 5
Stages 1 : 2 : 3 : 5 : 4

Notice that Stage 1 is common to all possible teaching sequences. This is because good footwork and basic body awareness are essential to the development of safety and confidence and must therefore come first.

If the group is active and lively it might be better to begin with *Locomo-*

I (*above*) *Total involvement* during the exploratory stage of a new theme – (*St. Cuthberts College, Auckland*).

(*below*) *Informality* provides a relaxed working environment and encourages variety and independence.

II Moving . . . into . . .

Counter-balance

One way out!

III (*above*) Asymmetrical shape and symmetrical balance.

(*below*) Group work: Symmetrical and asymmetrical balance.

IV & V Extracts from partner sequences illustrating:

(*top*)   Counter-balance.

(*centre*) Receiving and transferring partner's weight.

(*bottom*) Counter-tension.

VI   *Assisted balance*

(*top right*) Preparing to take weight on to hands on the Olympic beam.

(*bottom left*) Is this counter-balance?

Raising
partner's weight.
Note stable
base and straight
back position
in this strong
lifting action.

VIII *Flight* (*above left*)　　Feet to feet.
　　　　(*above right*)　　Final phase of a *Giant Cartwheel with a quarter turn over a box.*

(*below*)　　Final phase of a group sequence based on contrasting acceleration and deceleration. Back handspring (centre) provides 'climax' in acceleration. All finish simultaneously.

tion before *Weight Bearing.* Adapt your selection of teaching material according to the type of group. **Do not feel restricted to any one sequence of material.** Once you have covered Stage 1, select your teaching material using variety of progression.

Examples of tasks for both Movement Training and Apparatus have been centred around Basic Flight with weight being taken on either feet alone or combination of feet and hands. This is to prevent too much variety causing confusion. The teaching methods, the type of tasks set, the arrangements of apparatus which have been illustrated throughout this section can be used in any theme.

SECTION 2: Further Progressions

1 Body Shape.
2 Balance.
3 Emphasis on Aspects of the **SPACE FACTOR.**
4 Emphasis on Aspects of the **TIME FACTOR.**
5 Emphasis on Aspects of **FLOW.**
6 Combining Aspects of the Movement Factors.

1 Body Shape
The body can be: Curled and Stretched.
                       Symmetrical and Asymmetrical.
                       Twisted.

In setting tasks, emphasis can be placed on the *whole body*, weight on arms or on leg work.
Curling and Stretching
Example Tasks
  (i) Travel across the floor showing curling and stretching movements. (I)
 (ii) Take weight on to *one part* of the body, stretch, change weight so that it is supported on a *second part*, curl. Repeat sequence. (L)
(iii) Take weight on part of the body, curl, stretch out as far as possible in any direction, return to first curled position, stretch out in another direction, return to first curled position. (L)
(iv) Curl and stretch while balanced on your arms. (L)
 (v) Do a Handstand . . . Forward Roll. (D)
Symmetry and Asymmetry
If the body is divided by an imaginary vertical line, there will be corresponding parts on either side.
Symmetrical Movement is concerned with the use of **LIKE** parts of the body, **simultaneously** and **in the same way,** e.g. Taking weight from two feet to two hands, to two shoulders, to two knees, to two hips.

Asymmetrical Movement is concerned with the use of **UNLIKE** parts, at **different times,** in a **different way,** e.g. Weight transferred from one knee, to one shoulder, to one knee to one foot.

Example Tasks
  (i) Travel and show symmetrical use of hands and feet. (L)
 (ii) Make a sequence showing symmetrical use of at least two parts of the body. (L)
(iii) Travel on hands and show asymmetrical use of the hands. (Refer to Section 1, Stage 2, 4.) (L)
 (iv) Show a symmetrical weight-bearing position followed by an asymmetrical weight-bearing position. (I)
  (v) Show a sequence of movement which combines symmetry and asymmetry. (I)
 (vi) Take weight from right knee to left shoulder to left knee to right shoulder. (D)
                or
(vii) Take weight from right knee to left shoulder to right shoulder to left knee. (D)

Twisting
Twisting occurs:
  (i) When *part* of the body *initiates movement* with a *twist* and is followed by the *rest of the body*.
 (ii) When *part* of the body *remains fixed* and remaining part *twists around that fixed point*.
(iii) When one part of the body *twists* in a *contrary direction* to the other.[1]
    You might be able to help your group by suggesting that they achieve a change of direction and finish movements facing a different way.
e.g. Face forwards, take weight on to hands, lift feet off the floor and return to feet so that you are facing the opposite way. (L)
i.e. a twist at the hips will enable the change of direction to be made.

Methods
Example Tasks

Direct
Fix one hand on the floor and allow the rest of the body to move around that fixed hand. Twist round as far as possible, retrace steps unwinding the twist to end up at the original starting place.

Indirect
Find other parts which may be fixed and see how far the rest of the body can twist moving around those fixed parts.

[1] I.L.E.A., op. cit., p. 32.

Limited
Take weight on hands or shoulders, when weight is supported, twist at
the hips and bring feet back to the floor so that the body is facing a
different direction.

Using Apparatus
Tasks must be clearly defined on apparatus. Apparatus can be set in
straight lines as long as the task set is suitable to the theme of twisting,
e.g.:
Task on this *straight line* apparatus:
Using hands only on the box, arrive with your feet on the mat facing
the direction from which you came. (L)

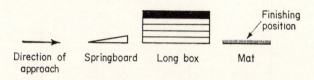

Direction of   Springboard   Long box   Mat
approach

Apparatus which is set in a more flexible way encourages more exploration and inventiveness because it presents a variety of approaches and
sometimes individuals will twist as a solution to negotiating a gap or angle
within the apparatus section.

Example Tasks
  (i) Using feet and hands to take weight, use beat board, horse, straight
      over the gap to the box and straight off on to the mat. (L)
          or
      Using any parts of the body to bear weight, use four pieces of the
      apparatus *without touching the floor*. (I)

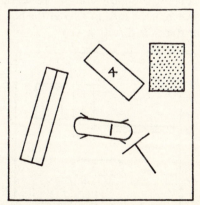

 (ii) Travel from beat board to box to mat or beat board, box to horse to mat, and show a twist from a position with feet above head before landing on the mat. (L)

or

Take weight on to three different parts of the body using three different pieces of the apparatus and show twisting. (I)

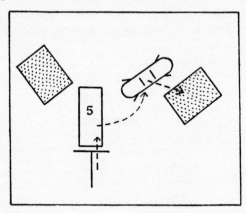

(iii) Transfer weight from horse to mat back to horse without stopping. (L)

or

Show a twist in passing between the pommels on the horse and a twist when leaving the box. (L)

or

Use any part of the body and apparatus section to show twisting movements. (I)

or

Show weight supported on arms on the horse, twist at the hips and arrive on the bench, use hands to go *over* the box and end up on the floor facing the opposite direction. (L)

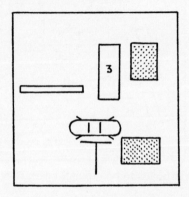

A group will often produce **turns** instead of **twisting** movements. You must help them to experience the *tension* which is part of the *twist* and *contrast* this with the *total lack of tension* in the turn, which is caused because the *whole body moves around as one.*

2 Balance

Balance is closely allied to weight bearing, in which positions of stillness are attained, but the supporting body surface area is reduced and finer control is needed to maintain a balance position. Use of unlike body parts can also increase the degree of difficulty, e.g. forearm supporting the body on a bench, one hand on the floor.

Balance involves:

(i) A base over which the body may balance, e.g. two hands, one shoulder.

(ii) The body's centre of gravity, which is the point about which the body weight is equally distributed. The exact location of the centre of gravity is relative to the changing position of the body parts.

(iii) The line of gravity, which passes vertically through the body's centre of gravity.

(iv) An area of balance, i.e. the distance it is possible to lean in any direction from the position of balance. The area of balance is limited and extends from the position of balance to a point at which the line of gravity falls *outside* the area of the base. At this point balance would be lost.

It is usually easier to maintain a balance position when:

(i) The area of the base is increased.

(ii) The centre of gravity is low.

(iii) The line of gravity, passing vertically through the centre of gravity, falls near to the centre of the base.

When introducing balance encourage your group to find out the answers to such questions as:

(i) How many parts of the body can provide a base over which the remainder of the body is held in balance?

(ii) What assists maintenance of balance?

(iii) What happens if weight is allowed to lean and assume a position outside the area of the base?

The area of balance varies with the type of base used. Encourage the group to explore these differences in order to increase their powers of judgement and muscular control when using a variety of bases on which to balance.

Example Tasks

(i) Using any part(s) of the body, find ways of balancing. (I)

(ii) Is it possible to balance over a base using three body parts simultaneously, reducing the base first to two parts and secondly to one part? (I)

e.g. This might produce a Headstand followed by a Handstand followed by a one hand balance. The movements could be done separately. If the group is highly skilled the movements could follow in quick succession, a push from the arms leading the body from Headstand to Handstand.

(iii) Choose three parts of the body on which to balance and link each balance position by overbalancing and rolling. (I)

(iv) Show balance using a part on the right, the left, then the right side of the body. (L)

(v) Balance on hands, another part of the body, and hands again. (L)

(vi) Show balance on hands, another part of the body, followed by a different balance using hands. (L)

(vii) Do an Arabesque to Handstand followed by a Shoulder Stand. (D)

When taking weight on hands within the theme of Balance, encourage the group to increase the *duration* of the balance. Take particular care to emphasize the *placing* of the hands on the floor or apparatus and the need to shorten the neck, stick out the chin and so lift the head when balancing on hands in the inverted position.

Consider methods of **Transference,** i.e. movements which may link one balance to another making continuity of movement possible. Balance itself is a part in a sequence which is **still,** but the body is actively involved in maintaining the balanced position through the exertion of **muscular tension**. It is similar to the dramatic pause in the theatre world. It contributes to the whole sequence so that it is possible to have continuity of movement when working on the sustained quality of balance and more sudden linking movements.

Linking movements could be:
>Rocking and Rolling.
>Step-like actions.
>Flight.
>Twisting.
>Pivoting.

3 Emphasis on Aspects of the Space Factor

Definitions:

Two types of space are used. They are:

The Personal Space which is the space immediately surrounding the body. This is called the Sphere of Movement.

The General Space which is the larger space of the gymnasium.

Movements can be carried out in the Personal Space and parts of the body may extend into that immediate space, e.g. Shoulder balance . . . feet extend upwards into the Personal Space.

Within this immediate space movements can be made towards and away from the centre of the body, e.g. curling and stretching.

Movements may be carried out within both the Personal and General Space at different **levels** and in different **directions.**

Using Different Directions
Example Tasks
(i) Can you travel and show change of direction? (I)

(ii) Can you travel forwards, backwards and sideways? (L)

(iii) Invent a sequence of movements on the spot in the Personal Space and travelling in the General Space using forwards and upwards directions. (L)

(iv) Invent a sequence showing two different directions. (L)

Pathways
Movements may describe various pathways or tracks, e.g. a square, straight line, a zig-zag, a circle, etc.

Example Tasks
(i) Go over the top beam, through the middle space under the lower beam, back through the middle space and over the top beam again. (L)

Q: What sort of track or pathway was described?

A: A figure of eight.

(ii) Invent a sequence of movements describing a square pathway. (L)

(iii) Is it possible to travel from one end of the bench to the other and over the adjacent box using a zig-zag pathway? (L)

(iv) Move freely over the apparatus and show a pattern. (I)

(v) Use a Gate vault followed by a Heave vault to show a pattern on the double Swedish beams. (D)

Pathways and Directions
In moving between points A and B which describe a direct, straight track or pathway, it would be possible to:

(i) Move in a forwards direction from A to B.

(ii) Travel with the back approaching point B first, i.e. backwards.

(iii) Travel with the side of the body facing point B and arriving at that point first, i.e. moving sideways.

(iv) Travel between points A and B using a combination of (i) and (ii) *or* (ii) and (iii) *or* (i) and (iii) *or* even (i), (ii) and (iii). These combinations would be completed between point A and point B.

When attempting to take change of direction as a theme, you must be careful to avoid producing movements which change **track** but not **direction.**

e.g. In describing a square track on the floor, individuals may use Forward Rolls to describe side one, Catsprings for side two, Bunny Hops along side three and Forward Rolls to complete the square.

In this sequence a square track has been described yet the body has used but one direction, i.e. forwards.

In describing such a square pathway or track it would be possible to change direction in a variety of ways.

Examples using (i), (ii) and (iii) as defined above:

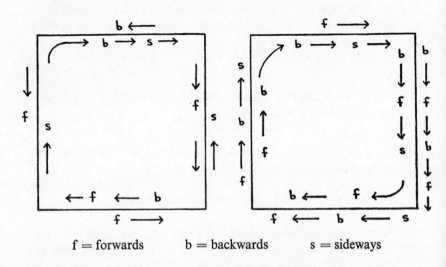

f = forwards   b = backwards   s = sideways

The diagram shows a variety of directions which could be used to describe a square track. Examples are illustrated on the outside and inside of the squares shown above. These are only some of the possibilities. There are many more.

Example Tasks:
(i) Is it possible to travel in a straight line using forwards, backwards and sideways directions?
(ii) Using a variety of movements to describe a triangular track on the floor, emphasize two different directions.

Twisting assists change of direction. When twisting the body usually begins the movement facing one way, ends it facing another and in this way enables the body to negotiate corners.

Levels

Example Tasks:

(i) Can you travel keeping contact with the floor so that movements are at a low level? (L)

(ii) Travel and show two different levels of movement. (L)

(iii) With weight on hands, show two different levels for feet. (L)

(iv) Invent a sequence in which the first movement is low, the second high and the third low. (L)

(v) Can you find three movements which show feet as the highest point off the floor? (L)

(vi) Travel anywhere, using any part of the body to take weight passing through a variety of levels. (I)

(vii) Show movements with feet high and feet low in the Personal Space and in the General Space.

(viii) Invent a sequence to show low level movements in the Personal Space and high level in the General Space. (L)

The Medium level can occur on apparatus such as double Swedish beam, but is not often used in Floor Work. If it is it mainly produces Cartwheel actions or bridge-like shapes, in which feet are raised and become the highest point off the floor.

Flexible and Direct

Movements between any two points A and B may be *flexible* or *direct*. Points A and B represent any one of the following:

(i) One weight bearing position to a second, e.g. shoulder stand to a standing position.

(ii) Two points on the gymnasium floor.

(iii) Two points on apparatus, e.g. one end of the box or beam to the other.

(iv) Two points linking apparatus, e.g. from balance beam to ropes or from springboard to box.

Direct movement describes a straight line pathway from A to B and is economical because it takes the shortest possible route. Often Direct movement has a sudden, almost urgent, quality. However, it can be slow, e.g. a Forward Roll describes a direct pathway but can be performed slowly or suddenly. A Through vault over the pommel horse can be performed quickly or slowly and can even be arrested midway, the body being supported above the pommel horse in a well held *L* shape before the vault is completed. A Thief vault describes a direct pathway. There can be no doubt about its sudden quality. The variable Through vault and the sudden Thief are both direct.

It is possible to take a movement theme of *Direct* with *change of speed* and so combine an aspect of Space with an aspect of Time.

Flexible movement describes a more extravagant pathway between points A and B. It meanders, producing curved, twisted and zig-zag spatial patterns. Flexible movement tends to be slow, the individual's sustained effort permitting her to *savour* each part of the movement. In the same way that direct movement can be slow, so flexible movement can be performed with a sudden quality, e.g. Screw vault.

Usually, individuals have a preference for slow or quick movement. Indirect tasks will enable individuals to exercise that preference. If you wish the group to experience different speeds, you will need to set direct or limited tasks. You could set a theme which contrasts *sudden direct* with *sustained flexible* movement.

It is always interesting to observe which girls prefer to move *directly* and which *flexibly*. Most have a preference and it is often indicative of personality, e.g. the direct, forthright individual often selects direct movement.

4 Emphasis on Aspects of the Time Factor
Rhythm
Most individuals have their own innate sense of rhythm. You can suggest to the group that they attempt to invent a sequence of movement which shows a distinct rhythm *or* you can *restrict* them initially to your own pre-selected rhythm, e.g.:

> Quick-slow-slow-quick
> *or*
> Slow-slow-quick-quick-quick-slow

It is usually more valuable for the group members to evolve their own characteristic rhythm and to extend experience of the variety of rhythms through the medium of partner work.

Emphasize the contrast between the sudden quality of the quick movements and the sustained quality of the slow movements. This sort of work can augment interest in Basic Flight work and in taking weight on hands or other parts of the body, and can assist in achieving continuity of movement.

Contrasting Slow and Quick Movements
(*a*) The *whole* body can move quickly or slowly.
(*b*) Part or parts of the body can move quickly or slowly. Parts moving quickly can provide a *climax* point of accent within a sequence.

Acceleration and Deceleration
This aspect of Time, requires finer grading in changing speed. The group

could be allowed to invent sequences at floor level, which show a series of movements accelerating in pace and, having achieved *maximum speed*, gradually decreasing in pace until the sequence finishes very slowly. This grading of speed can be particularly valuable in assisting Flight on to, off and over apparatus and deceleration can contribute to the safe recovery following movements of Flight.

Do **not** introduce the Time Factor until movement sequences are well performed. You may find it helpful to allow members of the group to perform their sequences slowly or quickly throughout, *before* asking them to show *change* and contrast of speed.

5 Emphasis on Aspects of the Flow Factor
Aims

 (i) To achieve Continuity of Movement.
 (ii) Ability to **arrest** movement and produce *Bound flow*.
(iii) Awareness of *Successive Flow*, i.e. effort passes through one part of the body to other parts in succession so that on completion of the movement several parts have been involved, possibly even the whole body.
(iv) Awareness of *Simultaneous Flow*, i.e. the **whole** body moves at the same time, e.g. as in a jumping action.

Free Flow is concerned with movement which is difficult to stop and this is not encouraged because it could be dangerous.

The nearest we can hope to get to *Free Flow* is Continuity of movement. Work at Continuity and later develop an ability to arrest and continue movements at will. To be able to arrest movement is particularly important when working on *Locomotion*

The opposite to *Free Flow* is *Bound Flow* which is concerned with the ability to be able to arrest movement. This is particularly important when working on Balance or combining Weight Bearing and Transference of Weight. To assist Continuity of movement on apparatus, you could restrict the group to using a *sequence of apparatus*, e.g.:

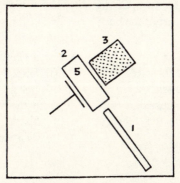

(i) Use box, mat and box again as quickly as you can (2–3–2).
(ii) Use bench, box and bench again changing from one to the other as smoothly as you can (1–2–1).
(iii) Use mat, box and mat again showing an even pace (3–2–3).

When using apparatus in a specific order, it is possible to set a general task which will cover a variety of apparatus, e.g. Wherever you are, use one piece of apparatus, use a second and quickly return to the first piece, i.e. 1–2–1.

6 A classification of the integral parts of movement in relation to the factors time, weight, space and flow.

All the Movement Factors are present in every movement. The Educational Gymnastics teacher encourages the group to emphasize one or more aspects of these factors. Take a look at the following movements: A **Forward Roll** followed by a **Handstand.** This is a short and easily repeated sequence.

The Forward Roll

1 *Time Factor*
  (i) Slow or quick.
  (ii) Gathering speed at the end to facilitate lift into Handstand position.

2 *Flow Factor*
  (i) Continuous, e.g. probably one foot leading the other to ease the transition from floor to raised Handstand position.
  (ii) Successive, i.e. quick change of weight with effort passing through one part of the body to another.

3 *Space Factor*
  (i) Pathway . . . forward.
  (ii) Level   . . . low.
  (iii) Shape   . . . curled.
  (iv) Travelling in the General Space.

The Handstand

1 *Time Factor*
  (i) Quick beginning and stillness in balance position.

2 *Flow Factor*
  (i) Bound flow, i.e. movement is arrested to show held position of stillness and balance.

3 *Space Factor*
  (i) Direction . . . Upwards.
  (ii) Level   . . . Medium, with feet high.
  (iii) Shape   . . . Stretched in balance, curved in preparation

4 *Weight Factor*
(i) *Heavy* ... relaxed lowering of
body weight with gravity
helping.

(iv) Travelling upwards in the
Personal Space.

4 *Weight Factor*
(i) Emphasis is on Stillness
which necessitates the conscious exertion of muscular
tension to hold the balance
position.
(ii) Use of gravity in returning
feet to the floor with *give* of
the knees in landing.

7 Combining Aspects of the Movement Factors: Time, Space, Weight and Flow
(i) Try combining *two aspects* of *one factor*.
(ii) Try combining one aspect of Time with one aspect of Space, e.g.:
(a) Move quickly in the General Space and slowly in the Personal Space.
(b) Show rhythm using different levels.

Following work on Basic Flight, select ideas freely from Section 2 according to the progress and interest of the group. You might introduce change of speed when attempting the combination of *Weight Bearing* and *Transference of Weight*. You could introduce *Rhythm* when working on *Locomotion* or you might extend work on *Balance* and *Transference of Weight* to *Contrast* work, showing *Bound* and *Continuous Flow*.

If individual work has reached a satisfactory standard, i.e. everybody has movement ideas and has invented a sequence of movements which are suitably linked and which answer the task, you could consider extending the work to partner work, or work in threes.

8 Visual aids to combining aspects of the movement factors

Combining Aspects of Weight and Flow

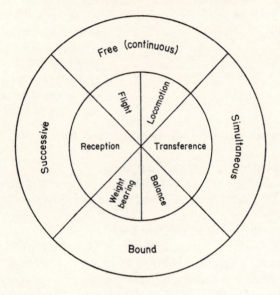

Examples of possible combinations:

  (i) Reception with successive flow.

 (ii) Weight bearing and bound flow.

(iii) Flight and locomotion with continuous flow.

(iv) Flight and transference with successive flow.

 (v) Simultaneous flow in flight with bound flow in balance.

Combining Aspects of Time and Weight

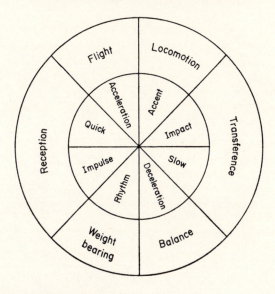

Examples of possible combinations:

  (i) Locomotion and acceleration.
 (ii) Locomotion and rhythm.
(iii) Flight and reception with accent.
 (iv) Weight bearing and flight with impact.
  (v) Weight bearing and transference with quick and slow.
 (vi) Flight and balance with acceleration and deceleration.

Combining Aspects of Weight and Space

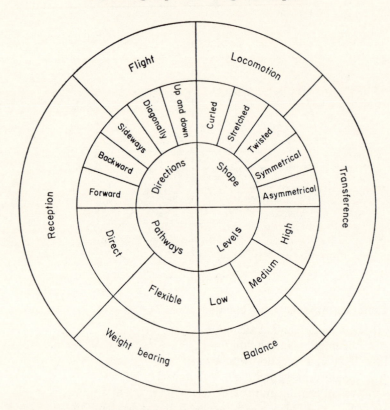

Examples of possible combinations:
  (i) Locomotion with contrasting levels, i.e. high and low.
 (ii) Balance with symmetrical and stretched shape.
(iii) Weight bearing and transference with twisted shape.
 (iv) Flight, forward direction with high and low levels.
  (v) Locomotion with direct, curled and stretched shape.
 (vi) Weight bearing and asymmetry with direct locomotion.
(vii) Locomotion, balance and flight with symmetrical shape.

Combining Aspects of Time and Space

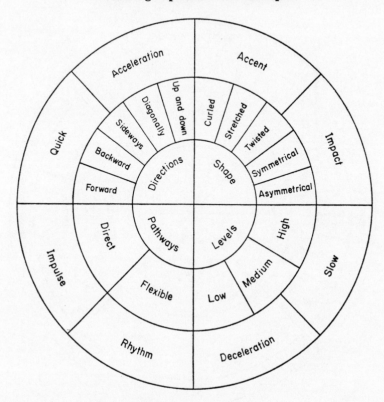

Examples of possible combinations:

   (i) Acceleration with symmetrical shape.
  (ii) Direct and flexible with accent.
 (iii) Curled and stretched with rhythm.
  (iv) Direct with slow and quick.
   (v) Symmetrical and twisted with high and low.
  (vi) Sideways and backwards with acceleration.
 (vii) Impact with symmetry.
(viii) Impulse with stretched and twisted.

Combining Aspects of Time, Weight, Space and Flow

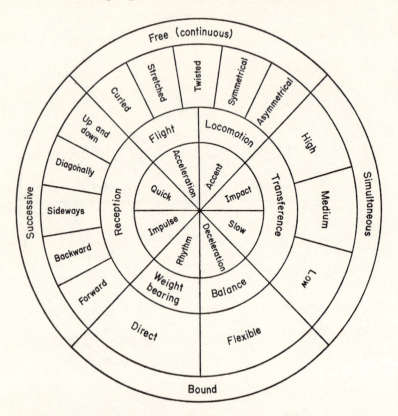

Examples of possible combinations:

(i) Direct and flexible, high and low, accent.

(ii) Locomotion, sideways and forwards, symmetrical and asymmetrical shape.

(iii) Balance and transference of weight, curled and stretched, quick and slow.

(iv) Locomotion, successive flow, curled and stretched.

(v) Weight bearing and locomotion, successive flow, symmetry, accent.

(vi) Flight and locomotion, high and low, direct, impact.

(vii) Locomotion, direct and flexible, successive flow, rhythm.

(viii) Flight and reception of weight, simultaneous and successive flow, symmetry, acceleration.

(ix) Weight bearing and balance, successive and bound flow, stretched, accent.

(x) Weight bearing and transference of weight, high and low, twisted and symmetrical.

(xi) Locomotion and flight, impulse and impact.

(xii) Weight bearing and locomotion, direct and flexible, quick and slow.

SECTION 3: Advanced Work

1 Combinations of Themes
Examples: Body shape and *change of direction.*
Flight showing *continuity* and *bound flow.*
Balance and *transference of weight* emphasizing *body shapes.*
Flight and *change of levels.*
Locomotion with variety of *shapes* and *directions.*
Any number of combinations are possible. Select your own.

2 Assessment of the Relationships between Movement Themes
Examples: Q: How does asymmetrical movement assist change of direction?

A: Movement is more flexible in its pathway and allows more change of direction to take place.

Q: How is loss of balance connected to change of level?

Q: Does symmetrical movement describe a direct pathway?

3 Losing and Regaining Balance
In more advanced work, you might introduce a theme which involves gaining balance and purposefully losing that balance.

(i) Balance might be *lost* by suddenly tucking up as in Front Support position on a beam or bar, followed by a tuck and Forward Circle over the beam or bar.

(ii) It might be *lost* by extending the weight of the body, so that the centre of gravity falls outside the area of the base supporting the body, e.g. Gate Vault.

(iii) It could be *lost* by twisting out of the inverted balance as when balancing in the inverted position on ropes.

4 Flight
In addition to the Basic Flight off feet to hands, Flight work of a more advanced nature can be done if the following are considered:
Turning in Flight
Diagonal Flight
Flight using movements which travel around the horizontal axis, e.g. a Front Somersault.[1]

[1] Refer to Chapters 11 and 12 in *Teaching Gymnastics* by E. Mauldon and J. Layson. op. cit.

SECTION 4: Extensions

1 Partner Work

Partner work augments interest because:

  (i) An individual may increase her *movement vocabulary*, e.g. through copying involved in *mirror* and *matching* sequence work.

 (ii) Through sequences which involve matching movements, an individual may experience innate movement quality which differs from her own. For example an individual whose characteristic movement quality is *sudden* may be placed in a sequence situation which demands *sustained* movement.

(iii) Socially, an individual learns to tolerate and appreciate another's movement skill and inventiveness.

(iv) Potential leadership may be discovered and encouraged.

 (v) Use of characteristic movement quality can be encouraged and the individual's ability to adapt increased.

     e.g. It would be possible for individuals to work using their own natural quality of movement in sequences in which **time** is the only partner limitation, i.e. partners simultaneously begin and end sequences but are free to select their own individual movements. Partner work in which partners are more dependent upon each other, as in supporting and obstacle work, would require sensitive adaptation of speed and body shape on the part of one or both individuals.

(vi) It develops the powers of observation and constructive criticism.

(vii) It increases accuracy of performance.

Types of Partner Work

  (i) *Matching* movements working side by side.

 (ii) *Mirror* work, i.e. working opposite one another as though looking into a mirror.

(iii) *Follow Me* work, i.e. copying pathway and exact movement, or copying pathway only or copying pathway and movement idea.

     e.g. Travelling the same pathway as partner, if partner takes weight on to her hands, to copy the *idea* of *weight on hands* but **not** the *same movement*.

(iv) *Contrast* work, e.g. contrasting shapes, levels, speeds, directions, etc.

 (v) *Related by Time* using *individual movements*, e.g. both begin and finish at the same time, but movements *within* the sequences are individually invented and performed.

(vi) *Canon* work, i.e. Number 1 moves and completes movement and Number 2 follows on starting just as the previous movement is completed by her partner. Movements can be the same *or* different.

(vii) *Making Obstacles* for partner to negotiate.
    Types: Static
           Moving
(viii) *Supporting Partner*
    Types: Passive, i.e. no active assistance is given, e.g. as in the support position of leap frog.
           Active, i.e. supporter **actively** lifts and assists partner to move or balance.
(ix) *Balance*
When taking a theme of Balance with partners pose such questions as:
  (a) Is it possible to balance on your partner using her as an active support?
  (b) Is it possible to balance against your partner using her as a passive support?
  (c) Is it possible to balance on corresponding parts, e.g. hands, using unlike surfaces on partner as a base of support, e.g. one knee and one foot?
(x) *Counter-tension*
To achieve Counter-tension partners must grip and pull strongly away from each other. To achieve a position of equilibrium the pulling forces must be equal. Partners may grip with *like*, e.g. hands, or *unlike* parts, e.g. leg(s) and hand(s).

It is interesting to decide how the tension may be dissolved. Can one partner initiate the release of tension by *letting go*? When partner A releases the tension by *letting go* partner B will move away from the gripping position, her movement following the line of her own pull. What happens to partner A who initiated the break in tension? Does her consequent movement logically follow in the direction of increased pull towards her partner? What difference would it make if the release were gradual rather than sudden? Does this affect the consequent movement?

When a position of Counter-tension is established on apparatus, partner A, by gradually relaxing her grip, could assist partner B to lower her weight from apparatus to floor. By increasing her pull she could assist partner B to raise her weight.

In group work, Counter-tension can be used in a theme which emphasizes pattern and accent. Patterns can be established as the group meets to set up positions of Counter-tension, and accent can be produced when tension is simultaneously released, or a series of accents can be emphasized as the release of tension is *staggered* throughout the group.

(xi) *Counter-balance*

To achieve Counter-balance partners lean towards each other until contact is established and partners can maintain a position of equilibrium. Using Counter-balance it is possible for individuals to balance at angles which would normally cause loss of balance. e.g. Two partners, each performing a Handstand back to back, could allow their bodies to lean away from the vertical position towards each other so that their feet make contact forming an arch. Normally feet held at such an angle would result in loss of balance.

or

Partners standing a few feet away from each other could raise their hands to shoulder level and allow themselves to *fall* towards each other until hands contact. Pressure which is proportionate to their different weights exerted between their hands will produce a position of equilibrium.

Counter-balance can be used to *raise* the body weight.

e.g. Partners, crook-sitting on the floor back to back, exerting suitable pressure against each other and simultaneously pushing from the feet can rise to a standing position without using the hands.

(xii) Emphasizing *pathways* or *patterns* on the floor and apparatus.

Examples: Movement towards and away from partner.

Movement towards and passing partner.

Movement to show a square pattern.

Movement to show a figure of eight.

When using movements based on meeting and parting or meeting and passing, to emphasize pattern, partners can:

(*a*) Travel towards each other, meet and travel back to their separate starting places.

(*b*) Travel towards each other, meet and travel away from each other to a different space.

(*c*) Travel towards each other, meet, and passing each other travel to a new space.

(*d*) Travel towards each other, meet using a support position, dissolve the support position and travel away from each other.

(*e*) Travel towards each other, at the point of meeting partner A provides an obstacle for partner B to negotiate before travelling in opposite directions.

In (*a*), (*b*) and (*c*) no contact is made. Contact is made in (*d*) and could be involved in (*e*) if the obstacle were also actively supporting, e.g. partner A lying on her back to support partner B as she does a handstand over her.

All these types of partner work can be transferred to small and large apparatus and can be combined, e.g. contrasting levels or shapes with supporting, *or* contrasting directions with obstacle partner work. Various combinations can be used. Select your own.

The stage at which partner work may be introduced will vary from group to group. Even between apparently comparable groups, there can be marked differences in the level of skills ability and social awareness. These differences make it difficult to generally advocate the introduction of partner work at any specific time. An appropriate time for its introduction can only be considered in relation to the experience and social awareness of the group in question.

Usually, primary school children enjoy individual work. They need constant individual activity. However, it is possible for children at the top of this age-bracket, to successfully produce the more simple varieties of partner work, e.g. 'matching' or 'follow me'. During their first year at the secondary school, eleven-year-olds are usually individualistic in their approach to the new environment. Initially, they are enthusiastic, even anxious, to prove themselves. Having achieved a degree of independence within the new environment, they sometimes independently begin to practise 'matching' pair movements or attempt to support each other. This indicates an increased social awareness. It reflects the need to share independently discovered movement ideas and willingness to co-operate in order to achieve specific skills or sequences of movement. It indicates the need to lead or follow and implies willingness to combine in appraising results. Spontaneous, independent pair movements can be a sign that partner work could be successfully introduced. However, it is not always necessary to wait for these signs to appear before introducing it. Providing the group understands the movement theme, sensitive timing in introducing partner work can precipitate the development of social awareness. It is unlikely that partner work will succeed, if the majority of the group has not yet achieved a measure of independence in working on the selected theme.

In introducing partner work, consider whether the work selected is suitable to the experience, skills ability and physical strength of the group, e.g. if you wish to increase individual variety within the group, you might select partner work which involves 'matching' or 'canon', using different movements. Such limitations can assist individuals to produce movements which are not usually in their movement repertoire. You must consider the degree of difficulty involved in the work, e.g. individual balancing skill would be a prerequisite for Counter-balance partner work.

When supporting is involved, ensure that partners are suitably matched in size. Instruct the group not to move over or against 'passive' supports until the supporter has assumed a braced position and is ready to receive her partner's weight. Teach correct lifting techniques for active support work. At the introductory stage of advanced work, it may be necessary to have an individual 'spotting' ready to support her partner, e.g. a sequence involving handspring or backward walkover. If so, emphasize the necessity for both 'spotter' and performer to plan exactly when and where the supported movement will occur. Be sure the 'spotter' knows the correct catching technique. If one partner cannot dispense with the 'spotter', it would be possible to incorporate supporting into the sequence without breaking continuity.

2 Group Work

This is an extension of partner work and groups can consist of three, four, five or six people. Subdivisions within the group can be varied according to the type of work being done. When working, for example, in a group of six the following might be possible:
e.g. 4 and 2 could be used for contrast work. It could be used to allow two people to travel over four constantly moving obstacles.
3 and 3 could be used for sequences showing meeting and passing or parting, or obstacles and supporting work, perhaps interchanging the supporter and *supported*.
6 working one after the other in *Canon* with identical *or* different movements.

Apparatus
This should be arranged to support the theme.

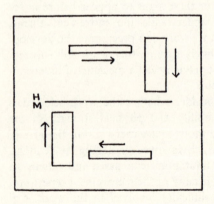

This apparatus might be used to suggest a square track over apparatus, or for contrasting levels and directions.

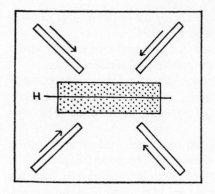

This apparatus might be used to suggest movement towards and parting or passing. The mat area might suggest low moving obstacles for others to negotiate whilst using the high beam.

Group Mechanics

(i) *Working in Threes*

Within the group of three, divisions might be:

$$2 + 1 \qquad 3 \times 1 \qquad 3$$

Two and One is a formation which lends itself well to showing contrast in levels and directions, to supporting and moving obstacle work. It may also be used to describe patterns on the floor and apparatus.

Three times one formation lends itself to a variety of independent movements. Individuals are simply bound by time contriving to begin and end their movements simultaneously. Contrast in levels, directions and shapes could be emphasized.

Three working together might produce sequences based on matching movements, *Canon, Mirror* and *contrast* shown in *unison*.

(ii) *Working in Fours, Fives and Sixes*

Within the group of four, division might be:

$$2 + 2 \qquad 4 \times 1 \qquad 3 + 1$$

Within the group of five, division might be:

$$2 + 1 + 2 \qquad 5 \times 1 \qquad 4 + 1$$

Within the group of six, division might be:

$$2 + 2 + 2 \qquad 4 + 2 \qquad 3 + 3$$
$$4 : 2 \times 1 \qquad 2 : 4 \times 1 \qquad 6 \times 1$$
$$3 : 3 \times 1$$

Multiple sign indicates individual work within the group framework, e.g. 4×1 indicates four individuals working independently.

Contrast Work in Partner and Group Work

When working on Contrast consider using:

Individuals working separately to show contrasting shapes, levels, speeds, directions, etc., beginning and ending the sequence together, but carrying out their own individual movements.

Both or all working to show one level, shape, direction or speed *changing* at the same time to show the opposite. Movements match.

Both or all working to show one level, shape, direction or speed using their own movements, i.e. *not* matching, changing after a predetermined number of movements to show the opposite, again using their own individual movements.

One or part of a group working on one aspect, the other or others working on the opposite aspect; change over to do the opposite. e.g. Number 1, or part of the group, begins with low movements, Number 2, or the other half or part of the group, begin with high movements, *change* and do the opposite. Movements could be the same or different.

Advanced Group Work

It is possible to increase the challenge of group work by moving the apparatus itself. *This could only be considered if a group were sensitive, controlled and experienced in the gymnasium.*

When working in threes, two could lift and carefully raise, lower, turn a bench on which a third member of the group could manipulate her weight.

Transition from moving bench to floor, possibly below and back to the constantly moving apparatus would need a high degree of skill and sensitivity. How to interchange and replace the moving individual on the bench would increase the challenge and interest. Mats could also be used as moving obstacles to be negotiated.

SECTION 5: College Workshops

Workshop sessions can be most useful to student teachers. They are often taken during refresher courses. Their main purpose is to provide the group with a little experience of several movement ideas. They also provide an opportunity for the group to examine the relationships which exist between the movement themes. Workshop sessions on *Accent, Impulse and Impact* might include the following:

PART 1: **Individual work on Accent**
Introduction **Accent** is achieved by:
> (i) moving one, or more than one part of the body suddenly, i.e. with a sense of urgency.
> (ii) moving the whole body suddenly.

Statement 1 Parts of the body can reach out into space and, by moving *suddenly*, give a sense of *arrival* in a specific body position.

Task   Take weight on shoulders with knees tucked close to the chest. *Slowly*, begin to stretch both legs upwards. Prior to achieving maximum stretch, *suddenly* thrust both feet upwards to emphasize your arrival in a fully stretched shoulder balance position. (D)

Extension   Find other parts of the body which could be used to emphasize arrival in a stretched body position. (L)

Statement 2   Parts of the body can slowly approach each other and suddenly withdraw immediately prior to contact, or they may slowly approach each other and suddenly *part as a result of contact.*

Task   Use different parts of the body to show meeting and parting with accent, e.g. right elbow and left knee. (I)

Extension   Slowly lower part of the body to the floor. On contact, suddenly withdraw that part of the body. Using different parts of the body, continue to contact and withdraw from the floor. Emphasize suddenness in withdrawal.

Statement 3   The sudden movement of the *whole body* can produce an *accent.*

Task   Use two Cartwheels and a Round-off to show a sequence which emphasizes locomotion and accent. (D)

Extension   Using whole body movements, construct a sequence to show *accent*. (L)

Assessment   Consider the following statements and questions:
  (i) Movement involving *accent* helps to develop body awareness.
  (ii) How could the theme *accent* increase variety of movement in the *Personal Space*?
  (iii) Movement involving *accent* helps individuals to experience and become aware of well-defined body positions.
  (iv) Could the theme *accent* help to develop resilience and sensitive reception of body weight? How could *accent* be applied to apparatus work to promote careful reception of weight and resilience?
  (v) How important is contrast in speed to producing *accent*?
  (vi) How could the theme *meeting and parting with accent* be extended to partner work?

PART 2: **Partner Work**

Theme   Meeting and parting with accent.

Statement   Using parts of the body or whole body movements, partners can move slowly towards each other and suddenly part either before contact occurs or as a result of contact.

Question 1   What happens when partners meet?

Answers
    (i) One partner actively supports the other.
    (ii) One partner provides an obstacle for the other.
    (iii) Partners establish positions of counter-balance.
    (iv) Partners establish positions of counter-tension.

Question 2   How can partners achieve accent?

Answers
    (i) Through *decisive* movement over obstacles.
    (ii) Through sudden, simultaneous movement away from positions of support, balance and counter-tension.

Tasks
    (i) Use counter-tension and active supports to show meeting and parting with accent. (L)
    (ii) Using counter-balance and obstacles, construct a sequence showing meeting and parting with accent. (L)
    (iii) Construct a sequence which emphasizes accent in a variety of ways. (I)

Extension   Group work involving:
    (i) Any one or combination of the above partner themes.
    (ii) Accent showing *chain reactions,* i.e. sudden movement of one member of the group initiates another member's movement, which initiates a third, etc.

PART 3: **Individual work on Impulse and Impact**

Statement   By combining accent with acceleration and deceleration, it is possible to achieve impact and impulse.

Definition   *Impulse* consists of an *explosive movement* causing a reaction which is expressed as a series of *decelerating movements.* *Impact* consists of a series of *accelerating movements* which end in a sudden climax, i.e. *accent.*
Impulse involves accent and deceleration. *Impact* involves acceleration and accent.

Tasks
    (i) Slowly perform a Cartwheel, accelerate into a Round-off followed by a Backward Roll, gather momentum to lift suddenly upwards into a Handstand balance. (D)

Initially, this could be practised in threes. Two students could lift the performer's ankles to assist her elevation from the roll into the Handstand balance.
Question: Is this impact or impulse?

(ii) Try to perform a Handspring, a Forward Roll followed by a Handstand. (D)

or

Try a Catspring followed by a Backward Roll to a knee balance. (D)
Question: Is this impulse or impact or neither?

PART 4: **Partner and group work on Impulse and Impact**

Example themes (i) Matching impulse and impact.

(ii) Impulse using different individual movements.

(iii) *Contrasting* impulse and impact.

(iv) Combination of acceleration, accent and deceleration, i.e. impact combined with impulse, using the accent of the former to initiate the latter.

Tasks (i) Construct a sequence which shows impulse or impact. (I)

(ii) Using a Handspring and other suitable movements, construct a sequence to show both impulse and impact. (L)

(iii) Use symmetrical movements to show impact.(L)

(iv) Use asymmetrical movements to show impulse. (L)

The legs have many functions in gymnastic movement. It would be possible to conduct a workshop session to examine these functions. The following outline might be considered:

ACCENT ON LEGS

1 *Propulsion and Locomotion*
 (i) Variety of footwork in travelling.
 (ii) Achieving height and distance, i.e. variety of take-offs.
(iii) Losing and gaining momentum.
2 *Reception*
 (i) Reception of weight from a height.
 (ii) Transference of weight.
3 *Balance*
 (i) Leverage.
 (ii) Initiating loss of balance.

(iii) Making gestures whilst the body is balanced.

(iv) Initiating twisting movements.

4 *Movement through Space*

  (i) Paths described by feet as they travel through space, e.g. the semi-circular pathway described by the feet in a Headspring, Forward Roll, Walkover.

 (ii) Contribution to symmetry and asymmetry.

(iii) Legs leading the body in specific directions, e.g. emphasizing arrival and departure when using apparatus.

5 *Legs in Support*

  (i) Using legs to support partner.

 (ii) Use of legs in lifting, i.e. apparatus or partner.

PART FOUR: Development, differences and difficulties

1 Development and Expansion

It is possible to expand and develop lesson content by considering the following progressions:

The Lesson
 (i) Apt proportion of lesson parts.
 (ii) Judicious use of indirect, limited and direct tasks, both separately and in combination.

The Body
 (i) Emphasis on the use of the legs.
 (ii) Emphasis on the use of arms.
 (iii) Emphasis on use of the whole body.
 (iv) Combinations of (i), (ii) and (iii).

Themes
 (i) Use of a basic theme, e.g. Weight Bearing.
 (ii) Combination of factors, e.g. Weight Bearing and change of level, i.e. Weight and Space factors.
 (iii) Assessment of the relationships between themes, e.g. twisting and asymmetry *or* loss of balance with change of level.
 (iv) Use of an advanced theme, e.g. flight around a horizontal axis *or* losing and regaining balance.

Methods *within* individual movement themes
It is possible to expand lesson content **within** a theme. A theme of Transference of Weight offers an opportunity to exploit the various methods by which transference of weight may be achieved, e.g. rocking and rolling, twisting, overbalance. There is a wealth of possible material to be gained from each of these methods. You could emphasize any one method and could increase the challenge by asking the group to find other methods. Later you could ask them to construct sequences which show a combination of different methods.

Similarly, turning, twisting, and flight can each bring about a change in direction. You might pursue each method and later set tasks which require a variety of methods to be used.

Apparatus Progressions
 (i) Small to large.
 (ii) Formal to informal *or* informal to formal.

(iii) Direct, indirect and some limited tasks set on the same formal *or* informal apparatus.

(iv) General tasks to specific separate tasks at each section.

It is possible for older, more experienced groups to:

(i) Arrange apparatus suitable for a theme set by the teacher.

(ii) Select a theme suitable for their own apparatus section which has been set by the teacher.

(iii) Arrange their own apparatus for a theme which has been selected by the whole class.

(iv) Use moving apparatus.

(v) Move freely between any two adjacent apparatus sections.

(vi) Move freely anywhere in the gymnasium, using all available apparatus and floor space.

(v) and (vi) develop a mature use of space.

Social Progressions

(i) Individual.

(ii) Partner.

(iii) Group.

The more simple forms of partner work are unison, mirror, following, meeting and parting *or* passing, and canon. The degree of difficulty can be increased by introducing support and obstacle, balance, contrast, or combinations of the various types of partner work, e.g. a sequence showing balance, obstacles, and meeting and parting.

METHODS OF LIMITATION

Theme: TWISTING

Type of Limitation	Example Tasks
(i) By restricting *pathway*.	Travel from ropes to box and back to ropes as quickly as possible.
(ii) By restricting the *order* of body parts to be used.	Use *hands* to take weight, *twist* and use a *second part* to take weight, *twist*, use *hands* again.
(iii) By restricting the use of parts to a *specific area* of the body.	Use a part located in the *top half* of the body to take weight, *twist*, take weight on a part located in the *lower half* of the body, twist to return to feet.
(iv) By stipulating the *direction* to be faced.	Arrive on the box facing the direction from which you came.

(v) By restricting the use to corresponding or unlike parts.

Fix two corresponding parts, e.g. hands or shoulders, twist to take weight on one single part, fix that part, twist, and return to feet.

(vi) By stipulating *track* or pattern.

Construct a sequence which describes a *zig-zag* track.

(vii) By stipulating *which parts* are to be *fixed*.

Take weight on *hands*, twist, weight on *shoulders*, twist, weight on *hands*, twist to return to feet.

Theme: BALANCE AND TRANSFERENCE OF WEIGHT, USING TWISTING

Type of Limitation	Example Tasks
(i) By restricting the number of balance positions.	Find a balance position, twist out of it, reassume the first balance position, return to feet.
(ii) By stipulating *which body parts* are to be used.	Balance on hands, twist, balance on one shoulder, twist, balance on one knee, return to feet.
(iii) By aiming at *variety* of balance positions when *using one particular body part.*	Balance on hands, twist, show a second balance on hands.
(iv) By restricting the use to *corresponding or unlike parts*.	Balance on corresponding parts, e.g. hands, twist, balance using unlike parts, e.g. one knee and one hand. Return to feet.
(v) By restricting the use to *corresponding parts in different areas* of the body.	Balance on corresponding parts located in the lower half of the body, e.g. knees, twist, balance on corresponding parts located in the upper half of the body, e.g. shoulders.
(vi) Limitation in the *size of the base*.	Balance on a single part, e.g. one shoulder, twist, balance on two parts (corresponding or unlike) e.g. stretched position supported on one knee and one hand.
(vii) By restricting the use to *inverted* balance positions.	Do a handstand, twist, return to feet. Take up another position with feet above head, twist and return to feet.

When introducing tasks, you must choose words which your group will understand. Any new terms such as *corresponding* should be explained. When setting a task such as (v) in the above table for the theme Balance and Transference of Weight, you would be wise to introduce each part separately and then ask the group to put the whole sequence together. You must be sensitive to the degree of difficulty and the potential understanding of the group.

2 Differences between Educational and Formal Gymnastics

Educational Gymnastics	Formal Gymnastics
1 Individuals work independently and usually produce variety of movements.	1 Rhythmical work is done in unison, or specific vaults are set and individuals follow one another.
2 Apparatus is set in a combination of ways, sometimes more formally and at other times, in conjunction with other pieces of apparatus.	2 Apparatus is usually one-piece, i.e. box longways.
3 As a result of 1 and 2, observation is more difficult.	3 Because of 1 and 2, teacher observation is easier.
4 Individuals can be active most, if not all, of the time.	4 There tend to be queues and less continuous activity.
5 This teaching approach takes into account the *differences* in people rather than the *similarities*.	5 This approach takes into account the *similarities* rather than the *differences* in people.
6 The teacher **stimulates** the group through the introduction of a movement idea, i.e. Theme.	6 The teacher directly imposes definite skills upon the group.
7 Three main methods of teaching may be used singly or in combination.	7 Direct method of teaching is used, e.g. stand feet astride, swing arms to the right, etc.
8 The individual, either when working alone or when inventing sequences with a partner or within a group, consciously contributes towards the lesson.	8 Emphasis is on the group receiving instruction. Contribution is made in the form of concentration, willingness, alertness, vivacity in response to the commands of the teacher. Exercises can become almost automatic and quite mechanical in execution.

9 Independence of thought and movement interpretation is encouraged.

9 Group timing and mass production of the same movement are imposed, particularly in the exercise section.

10 *Sequences* of movement are developed on the floor and apparatus.

10 There may be a *routine* of continuously performed exercises in the rhythmical work. Usually, single vaults are executed or one movement is encouraged, e.g. somersault between two ropes, astride vault over the box, etc.

11 The theme first explored on the floor is consciously and purposefully transferred to the apparatus.

11 Rhythmical exercises are divorced from apparatus work. No conscious effort is demanded of the group to apply the exercise work to the apparatus. Certainly the exercises might strengthen or increase suppleness of movement. In fact the teacher may consider the linking of exercise and apparatus work, but there is no conscious effort on the part of the group to do this.

12 Less teacher demonstration due to the method of extracting varied interpretations of tasks.

12 Usually more teacher demonstration.

13 Actual *muscular exercising* of various body parts is gained **incidentally** in the process of working out movement ideas within the theme, e.g. take weight from feet to hands and back to feet. Possible movements are: Catspring, Dive Roll, Handstand, etc.

  (i) All involve strong take-off from feet . . . use of leg muscles.

  (ii) All involve the body being curled and stretched . . . use of the spine.

13 More emphasis is placed on the *systematic exercising* of particular muscle groups, to develop strength and suppleness combined with a sense of rhythm.

Educational Gymnastics	Formal Gymnastics
(iii) Arms, legs and trunk have all been used.	
14 Challenge: The challenge is not so easily recognized because of the variety of activities and interpretations within the idea introduced by the teacher. The responsibility of assessment rests with the individual who is, however, prompted by the teacher. Certainly, a higher box, beam or new arrangement of apparatus may present further challenge, but because of the individual work it is the student herself who must constantly push herself to do her best.	14 Challenge: The challenge is usually more easily recognized in the form of increased height on apparatus or simply keeping time with the rest of the group and performing well within the restriction of group work.
15 The students are encouraged to consciously use mind and body to develop skills and solve movement problems. Through consideration of the integral parts of all movement, an awareness of not only **WHAT** the body is doing, but **HOW** it is doing it, develops.	15 There is an opportunity to learn through the process of imitation or direct coaching. The student knows **WHAT** the body is doing, i.e. swinging, jumping, arching . . . but *does not always understand* **HOW** the body is moving, because she has not been guided towards a *conscious awareness* of the integral parts of movement.

Each method presents its own challenge and therefore, attracts different personalities and age-groups. No one method can meet all needs of all people all the time.

3 Difficulties in Teaching Educational Gymnastics

There are *four* main problems involved in the Educational Gymnastics approach. Problems concerning the *student's approach* are:

(*a*) The constant repetition of the same movements and the development of a recurring sequence pattern.

Remedy – Suggest new approaches; use of a different part of the body;

another shape; another direction; possibly set apparatus in an entirely new way within the same theme.

(b) Inability of the individual to accept and respond to the constant subjective challenge, i.e. 'Is that as high as I can get?' *or* 'Were my legs stretched?'

Remedy – Watchfulness and timely prompting from the teacher to 'Reach higher' *or* 'Stretch legs', etc.

Problems arising from the *teacher's situation* are:

(a) Emphasizing variety for the sake of variety. Consider the value of repetition in relation to the needs of the class.

(b) Too much talk and not enough action. Consider that too much talk slows down the whole pace of the lesson and could cause the group to lose interest.

4 The Role of the Teacher

The teacher's role is more exacting, challenging and interesting than ever before! She must be able to:

1 Set tasks which offer every individual the opportunity to succeed.

2 Observe many actions simultaneously.

3 Divide her attention between group and individual coaching.

4 Be sensitive in timing the duration of lesson parts and the length of time to be spent over a series of lessons on any particular theme.

5 Be able to guide the group's powers of observation sufficiently well to stimulate interest and augment understanding.

6 Be sensitive to the fact that *invention* must be *balanced* with gaining *knowledge and understanding of skills* through the medium of *Direct coaching*, i.e. People sometimes like to be told what to do. Even the most inventive of us occasionally prefer to be directly told what to do, work at, aim for, etc.

7 Judge when and what to observe. In observing she must stress a definite point either by making a statement or by posing a question.

8 Use her voice in a way which is conducive to producing the desired response, i.e. in inventing sequences suggestions are made in a conversational tone and not in a crisp, direct, formal manner. Alterations in tone of voice can produce movements ranging from those showing speed to those involving smooth steady transition from one weight-bearing position to another.

9 Judge whether an individual is sufficiently challenged by the work and if not, consider means of remedying this, i.e. is the task too easy? Is the apparatus suitable to the task and theme? Make the necessary adjustments.

10 Be there to encourage the group to **enjoy** movement taking care not to become over-analytical, particularly in the initial teaching stages, when perhaps she is interested to see how themes may be developed.

5 Adaptation of Educational Gymnastics for Competition

It is believed that the enthusiastic response to Educational Gymnastics may, in part, be attributed to its lack of competition. There are people who are interested in the further development of gymnastics as a competitive sport. Within a school there may only be a few individuals who need and enjoy the stimulation of the challenges involved in competition. Their needs should be considered. A gymnastic club might be the answer. Possibly, more individuals would be interested in accepting the challenges of competition, if there were an element of choice.

Inter-house, inter-form and inter-year Games, Swimming and Athletics competitions are usually regular, popular features of the School Physical Education programme. It might be possible to encourage gymnastics as a competitive sport by holding an internal competition.

Amongst the following suggestions you will notice several points which are also common to formal competition. However, one very important difference is that specific movements, e.g. Headspring, Walkover, etc., are **not** required in either compulsory or voluntary sequences. Instead, in compulsory sequences, the organizer requires the competitor to illustrate a *specific movement theme.* In voluntary sequences the individual must use suitable movements to illustrate a specific theme which *she herself has chosen.*

When specific movement themes are set, an individual is required to *select independently* suitable movements. When selecting movements she will usually select those within her capabilities. The ability to select appropriate movements and to perform those movements with quality are the two main criteria involved. The competition organizer does not impose any degree of difficulty, except in the form of more advanced themes for more experienced competitors. However, an individual who is able to theoretically construct a more interesting sequence yet is prevented from practically realizing that sequence, through her inability to perform a particular movement, will practise that movement until it can be included in the sequence. This increased degree of difficulty and the self-discipline required to achieve it is **self-imposed.** Certainly, during practice sessions you might suggest certain movements but the individual has the choice of accepting or ignoring those suggestions.

When helping at practice sessions you should warn girls against the inclusion of favourite movements which do not illustrate the theme. You should encourage girls to sometimes include movements which are outside their usual movement repertoire.

Basic points in the following outline are included to assist those teachers who are not familiar with competition organization. Apparently obvious details have also been included because some misguided people may think that competition which allows the application of basic Educational Gymnastics concepts presupposes a rather *laissez-faire* approach. This type of competition requires teacher-imposed disciplines combined with self-discipline on the part of the competitors. An opportunity to make independent choice and to exercise self-discipline should in no way provide an excuse for lack of form.

1 Competition Outline
The competition could include:
  (i) A compulsory sequence on the floor.
 (ii) A voluntary sequence on the floor.
(iii) A compulsory sequence on the pommel horse or box.
 (iv) One voluntary vault on the pommel horse or box.
  (v) A voluntary sequence on the Olympic beam.
 (vi) A voluntary sequence on a Swedish beam,
                or
        A voluntary sequence on a section of informally arranged apparatus.

Floor Work
(a) Sequences to be invented.
(b) Sequences to be performed within a specific area, in which mats may be appropriately placed to suit individual requirements.
(c) A minimum and maximum time limit to be set, e.g. minimum 25 seconds, maximum 40 seconds.

Penalties
For exceeding time limits . . . loss of one point.
For using the floor space outside the specified area . . . loss of one point.
For lapses in memory, which cause the individual to lose her sense of direction thereby preventing continuity in performance . . . loss of one point.

When defining the judging system, intending organizers could refer to the International Gymnastic Federation's 'Code of Pointage'. They could select from it such points as may be relevant to the content and appropriate to the aims of the Competition they wish to run.

Types of Sequences to be performed
Compulsory, in which the theme is to be selected by the organizer(s). The theme selected should be a theme which has been covered within curriculum or club time, e.g.

Curling and Stretching (Body Shape).

Weight Bearing and Transference of Weight, combined with Changes of Speed.

Rhythm and Changes of Direction.

Voluntary, in which the competitor is allowed to **CHOOSE** from a collection of themes. A choice of four to six themes could be listed on the board. The choice given should take into account the age and experience of the group or individuals concerned.

Apparatus Work

Horse or Box

(a) Free choice of any *one* vault.

(b) Sequence of two movements travelling over the box or horse. (The floor may be used). The sequence to be based on the **SAME THEME** as in the *Compulsory* Floor Work.

Olympic Beam

    Voluntary Sequence, which is to demonstrate:

    Continuity, Rhythm, and Variety of Body Shape.

Swedish Beam

        Voluntary Sequence, which is to be based on a theme chosen by the competitor from the list of themes provided by the organizer(s).

           or

        A section of *freely* arranged apparatus, on which the competitor demonstrates a sequence of movements based on her selected theme, taken from the list of themes provided by the organizer(s).

        The Choice of Themes for Beginners might be:

           Curling and Stretching.

           or

           Different Directions, Levels or Shapes.

        The Choice for a more Experienced Group might be:

           Weightbearing, with change of speed.

           or

           Balance showing variety of body shape.

           or

           Locomotion showing different levels or rhythm.

This type of competition could be extended to inter-school matches. Obviously, staff concerned would need to meet to discuss suitable themes and method of assessment.

For purposes of internal competition, the New Zealand Gymnastic Association provides graded sets of movement sequences for floor work. In such a situation, you might substitute the relevant grade for the Compulsory Floor Sequence. Girls aged 16–18 might find it stimulating to invent floor sequences to suitably selected music. When working to music, the individual is restricted to a certain rhythm. It has been said that it is better for the individual to work using her own characteristic movement rhythm. However, the individual usually chooses music which gives scope to that natural rhythm.

The competitor might invent a movement sequence and, having chosen a piece of music, adapt her sequence, or she might listen to a piece of music and, having noted the crescendo or climax points and listened for suggestions of change of speed, moments of balance or elevation, she could construct her sequence accordingly.

To prevent her characteristic rhythm from being submerged you should allow her to choose her own music.

2 Judging

(a) To be carried out by two or three people.

(b) Each sequence to be marked out of twenty.

(c) The individual's total to be entered on a score sheet and contribute towards the team total.

Points to look for in Judging

(a) Poised beginning and ending to sequence.

(b) General awareness of body extension and position.

(c) Good continuity.

(d) Variety.

(e) Suitable selection of movements to illustrate the specific compulsory and voluntary themes.

(f) Originality in sequence construction, e.g. weight bearing and balance positions can sometimes be linked with more unexpected movements.

Part of the competition could include partner or group work. In this case you would have to assess timing. Sensitive timing is essential to partner and group work. Decisive arrival in various balance positions and timely changes of pattern and support contribute to successful team work. Partners or group members should complete the sequence at exactly the same time, unless the nature of the work renders this impossible. e.g. 'canon' work.

3 Competition Organization

If you decide to run a competition, be professional in your approach.

(a) Insist on gymnastic uniform.

(b) Allot separate spaces for the audience and the group of competitors.

(c) Insist that the audience remain silent whilst competitors are performing.

(d) Instruct your competitors not to commence their sequences until there is silence.

(e) Guide the competitors concerning suitable hair style and warn them against fidgeting with clothes during or at the end of a sequence.

(f) Supply the judges with large score cards which may be easily seen when held up at arms length.

(g) Appoint an individual to keep a large score sheet, which should be displayed on a board after the competition.

(h) During the competition keep the teams and audience informed concerning scores by appointing an individual to write *running totals* on a blackboard.

(i) Appoint a volunteer apparatus removal squad to facilitate the necessary apparatus changes.

(j) To maintain the pace and competitive atmosphere, announce the items and competitors' names yourself.

(k) Provide an award for the winning team.

(l) Provide specific times in which the various groups may practise their sequences. These practices should not be allowed to interfere with normal curriculum arrangements. Those who are really keen will practise at every available moment. Perhaps other staff might help to supervise practice times.

If a school were divided into five Houses and within each House, four year groups were each represented by four competitors, i.e. sixteen competitors in each House, as many as eighty students would be involved in actual competition. In addition, those helping with time-keeping, scoring and apparatus removals, would be contributing to the smooth running and success of the competition. The awe-inspiring image of competition for the very select few can be dispelled.

If Educational Gymnastics is completely new to your students and you feel that some need the challenge provided in competition, you should run a competition along the usual formal lines. Later, when Educational Gymnastics is more established, you might consider the value of including one section, or more based on Educational Gymnastics' themes. In any case, *competition should only be included for those girls who are interested and keen to participate.*

6   Summary

This material attempts to provide you with a broad outline of the principles, aims, movement factors and themes involved in teaching Educational Gymnastics. It is impossible to cover every aspect in detail. Of necessity, examples within the various themes have been reduced to a minimum. Most examples have been given with the sections on Basic Flight, Reception of Weight, Locomotion and Weight on Hands. You should transfer the *principles* of teaching method, arrangement of apparatus, stages of learning and general points concerning observation to *all* the themes.

If you are teaching more than one class within the same age-group, select a theme for each, but try to cover the same type of work with all by the end of the term or year. You might occasionally select the same theme for two classes, so that you may compare ideas and standard. No two classes work exactly the same way and you may see differences of approach to the theme. However, your teaching will remain spontaneous and vital if selection is varied.

Those teachers who take an inquisitive glance at Educational Gymnastics often become keen to try it themselves. Unfortunately they often crowd too much into one lesson, e.g. 'I want you to balance, change your weight, show different body shapes, and see if you can change level or direction.' If we were introducing young children to painting, I am sure our primary aim would be to give the children an experience and appreciation of colour. We certainly would not talk about 'Cubism' or 'Impressionistic Art', etc. We might progress to the relationships which exist between the different colours, e.g. yellow and red make orange. In a similar way both twisting and asymmetrical movement could be sampled. A progression might be to relate twisting and asymmetry to change of direction. Too much material will produce untidy, disappointing lessons which achieve little in any aspect of the theme.

Another common fault is an inexplicable tendency to rush through the stages of the lesson. It is important to allow sufficient time for students to achieve a good standard in their work.

One of the major criticisms levelled at Educational Gymnastics is its apparently nonchalant attitude towards safety. No such nonchalance exists. More freedom of movement is allowed because every teacher gives her class a thorough grounding in the ways in which the body weight can be safely received from different levels and positions. Some time is spent on achieving this ability to meet hard apparatus and floor surfaces with relaxation. Resilient recovery from the reception of weight is also emphasized. This safety training always comes first. Naturally, anyone who was not aware that such training had been given, would be perturbed at the free and independent movement which can be seen in any Educational Gymnastics lesson.

Sound teaching in reception and resilience in recovery is the main safety precaution. Another important safety factor is the students' ability to assess their own capabilities. Those who doubt their ability to perform specific movement skills will ask for help or simply decide not to attempt the movement in question. Accidents are more likely to occur when adults are over-ambitious for their students and impose their standards on the group. Other factors which contribute to safety are the teacher's own sense of anticipation and alertness in observation. People often mistake confidence for nonchalence!

Teachers sometimes underestimate the powers of perception students possess. *Movement* tasks often stimulate them to perceive several possible solutions to the problems. By extracting movement ideas, teachers are attempting to recognize and give full scope to those powers. When a student feels incapable of practically realizing her movement idea, she will usually hesitate or ask for help. You must be prepared to follow up the stimulus provided by assisting students to find solutions to difficulties which may arise. Some misguided people think that indirect teaching only requires the teacher to provide a stimulus to movement. The stimulus is but the beginning! You will be required to offer suggestions which assist students to answer the task you have set. Such suggestions may be given to the whole group or to individuals. They may initiate the students' work or supplement movement ideas which are partly formed or even well established. Sometimes you will be required to *actively* support or *directly* coach specific mechanical points necessary to skilled performance and understanding. The student who discovers *what* is wrong with her movement may need you to explain *why*.

The ease with which movement skill and quality may be achieved varies according to individual body build and aptitude. Educational Gymnastics recognizes that differences in ability make it necessary to provide an environment in which students, working within their own capabilities, primarily measure self against self. Therefore, progress must be assessed in relation to each individual's *initial* movement quality, skill and *confidence*.

This type of work is enthusiastically carried out in both Primary and Secondary Schools in England. Shirley Howard of the University of Michigan acted as the American co-ordinator for the second Anglo-American Workshop on Movement Education, held in England in July 1966. In her report she wrote the following statements concerning Educational Gymnastics:

First the individual development of each student is paramount.
Every student has many opportunities to experience satisfaction from successful use of his body. Thus, success contributes to the improved self-confidence of the student, enhances his self-image and provides a basis for his seeking more challenging tasks.[1]

[1] Shirley Howard, 'The Movement Education Approach to Teaching in English Elementary Schools,' *Journal of Health, Physical Education and Recreation,* January 1967, p. 31.

Creativity is encouraged because there is no single response to the problems.[1]

At the end of the report Shirley Howard wrote:

Selected reactions of the participants summarized the observations made in England and reveal their stimulating effect on the American delegation.

She quotes:

'The student learns to respect his own abilities as well as the abilities of others.'
'The movement approach seemed to draw out the shy, self-conscious child and lead him to other experiences.'
'Continuous activity was emphasized throughout the lesson.'
'All the children felt success in what they were doing.'
'The major contribution to learning is that movement education tends to develop a positive self-concept.'[2]

Reading will increase your intellectual understanding of the aims, themes and movement factors. Demonstrations and discussions can be valuable in augmenting both understanding and interest in Educational Gymnastics. But the **only way** to gain a **working understanding** of all that is involved in Educational Gymnastics is to **teach it.**

[1] Ibid.
[2] Ibid. p. 33.

RECOMMENDED READING

BABBITT, DIANE H. and HAAS, WERNER. *Gymnastic Apparatus Exercises for Girls*. New York: Ronald Press, 1964.
This provides an outline of beginning and intermediate skills on apparatus; primarily a formal approach but with some suggestions for exploration.

CAMERON, M. McD. and PLEASANCE, PEGGY. *Education in Movement: School Gymnastics*. Oxford: Basil Blackwell, 1963.
A guide for teachers of Educational Gymnastics.

INNER LONDON EDUCATION AUTHORITY. *Educational Gymnastics*. London: Inner London Education Authority, 1962.
Compiled by the Physical Education Inspectorate, this book defines movement factors and illustrates their application in movement themes.

LOKEN, NEWTON C. and WILLOUGHBY, ROBERT J. *Complete Book of Gymnastics*. 2nd. ed. Englewood Cliffs, N.J.: Prentice-Hall Inc., 1967.
Chapters 10–13 include an illustrated vocabulary of skills for floor work, vaulting, balance beam, even and uneven parallel bars.

MAULDON, E. and LAYSON, J. *Teaching Gymnastics*. London: Macdonald and Evans Ltd., 1965.
Every teacher involved in teaching Educational Gymnastics **must** read this book. It defines and discusses principles of movement and teaching method; it offers suggestions concerning the selection and arrangement of apparatus.

INDEX